LATE VICTORIAN

HOUSES AND COTTAGES

Floor Plans and Illustrations for 40 House Designs

DESIGNED BY

THE CENTURY ARCHITECTURAL CO.

DOVER PUBLICATIONS, INC.
Mineola, New York

Published in Canada by General Publishing Company, Ltd., 30 Lesmill Road, Don Mills, Toronto, Ontario.

Bibliographical Note

This Dover edition, first published in 1999, is an unabridged republication of the work originally published in 1897 by The Century Architectural Co. under the title *Modern Homes, A Collection of Practical Designs of Houses and Cottages*. In addition, nine advertisements from this book have been included in the new edition.

Library of Congress Cataloging-in-Publication Data

Modern cottages.
    Late Victorian houses and cottages : floor plans and illustrations for 40 house designs / designed by the Century Architectural Co.
        p.   cm.
    "First published in 1999, is an unabridged republication of the work originaly published in 1897 by the Century Architectural Co. under the title Modern cottages."
    Includes bibliographical references and index.
    ISBN 0-486-40490-0 (pbk.)
    1. Architecture, Domestic—United States—Designs and plans.   2. Architecture, Victorian—United States—Designs and plans.   I. Century Architectural Co.   II. Title.
NA7207.M63   1999
728'.37'0222—dc21   98–43893
                                                                  CIP

Manufactured in the United States of America
Dover Publications, Inc., 31 East 2nd Street, Mineola, N.Y. 11501

SEVENTH EDITION.

MODERN HOMES

1897

A COLLECTION OF PRACTICAL DESIGNS

——OF——

HOUSES AND COTTAGES.

DESIGNED, ARRANGED AND PUBLISHED

——BY——

THE CENTURY ARCHITECTURAL CO.,

ARCHITECTS AND SUPERINTENDENTS,

802 and 803 Mohawk Building, CLEVELAND, OHIO.

OUR COMPLETE AND ECONOMICAL ARCHITECTURAL SERVICE.

A FEW years ago it was nearly impossible to find competent architects who would design and prepare the working drawings and specifications of a $1,000 cottage, and their charge was not less than $100 ; for a $5,000 house not less than $250, and for houses of various costs not less than the pro rata charges thus indicated. These charges had the effect of a "prohibitive tariff", and the development of domestic architecture was much retarded ; architects were seldom employed for houses of low and moderate costs, and, as is well known, such houses were void of beauty and convenience. This company was formed to carry out the ideas of the building public, for any and all kinds of work embodying the useful with ornamental and advertise that complete drawings, specifications, etc., for anything from a $1,000 cottage (or even less), including consultations and advice, prepared by thoroughly competent architects would be furnished at a price within the reach of all. Progressive people have approved of our methods and an extensive patronage has followed, and now at the end of seven years, more have taken this prompt way than would seem creditable to many. The service has greatly improved, but the charges have not increased. For buildings of the lowest cost up to $25,000, and in fact up to any price our service is unquestionably the best as well as the least expensive. Thousands gratefully testify in the most positive terms to its merits after employing it.

FALSE ECONOMY.

The party to a lawsuit who acts his own lawyer, despite his want of legal training, is very unwise. Although his quarrel be just, his defeat is probable ; easily accomplished, it may be, with mere tricks of technical skill performed by the trained lawyer whom he opposes. The same may be said of the physician, etc. Equally unwise is the owner who determines to build without the important advantages of an architect's advice and aid. Without this advantage, the inevitable defeat awaits him of building a poor house at a cost that would have built a good one. Even if the owner wants no change of floor plans or exteriors from some other building or our designs, our knowledge of the best materials and various belongings of a house, which are continually changing, often better articles at a less price, coming into use, which enables us to revise or write specifications for the proposed structure that will unquestionably improve its appearance and convenience and reduce the cost as well. We prepare careful drawings of all floor plans, elevations and details, and write full specifications of the kind and quality of all materials to be used, also describing how the work shall be done. With everything so full and plain, there is an improved chance of getting a low bid and avoiding also extras, and giving every man that figures an equal chance. We advise and assist in making the contract, and at the start, during the progress, or at the end of the work, can be called upon for advice or inspection of work at any distance, and have saved many owners considerable money and insured them a better building after such trips. Not of the least importance is that the architect acts as arbitrator in matters of disagreement between the owner and contractor.

PROCRASTINATION.

Many delay until the last moment the placing of their orders for architectural work, which is wrong, as it does not give the client or architect the proper time to study, and develop the plans before completion. Many are also deterred from building by the warning often heard, "Estimates are unreliable." This is certainly true concerning many estimates, such as those given by incompetent or unprincipled men, but it is just as certainly not true of estimates made by reputable architects. The danger of deception as to cost is avoided by employing architects of well known ability and reputation. Figures we give with our designs are actual contract figures taken from buildings erected or about to be erected.

Needless delays are caused often by the owner's unsuccessful, because unassisted, search for a satisfactory plan, or to the impossible task he has given himself, or determining without expert advice, upon the merits of various systems of plumbing, heating, lighting, draining, etc.

The wife, daughter, mother or affianced, who will be mistress of the new house, is hard to please with building designs, as her sisters have been before her ; a critical requirement that has stimulated the most effective study and invention for the improvement of domestic architecture. Her ideal is pretty clearly pictured in her mind, but she is always "touching it up." Should she chance upon her latest ideal, she would straightway "touch it up ;" and be off again. She is progressive. It will help her (as well as progressive people) to know this ; she will never find a design that will quite fully satisfy her, very often wishing more than their means allow. Until all things are perfect, the most prolonged effort and the art of the most skilful designers can only make a near approach to perfect approbation ; with that limitation, sooner or later, a design must be accepted if the proposed house is ever to become a more substantial structure than an ever-changing creation of the fancy.

Consult the architect at once and see how quickly the deterring fear and the delaying causes will take wing. He is glad to help the owner from the very start, and his fee is not increased thereby, at least in this office. Concerning all undecided matters, we can give the owner at once the full information necessary for decision, which he had vainly attempted to acquire.

OUR SERVICE FOR CLIENTS AT ANY DISTANCE.

The adaptability of our plans and service to the most distant places need not be doubted by anyone taking the trouble to inquire of those who have employed us. In addition to regular drawings and specifications (all full and plain) made in duplicate, one set for contractors, and the other for your own use, so as to allow you to follow the work along. We send supplement, drawings and instructions which, with the owner's privilege of consulting us at any moment (by telegraph if necessary), fully answer for local superintendence. We equip the owner, wholly inexperienced though he be, with the knowledge that makes him a good superintendent.

We look up the best articles to specify, and establish the cost of building on such articles, so it is well to remember, do not let the contractor substitute something that is better or just as good, or equally so. If they are honest let them use what is specified, and in that way all have an equal chance in figuring.

It is a mistake to believe that an intelligent client cannot fully understand and carry forward the building of a house of low or moderate cost when aided by the drawings or written instructions (supplemented by further advice as needed) of competent architects, who keep steadily in view the fact that instructions are given an experienced man. The fact is, the best houses are built by such owners, for they will not pass anything that appears imperfect. If they are uncertain they ask the architect, who takes the utmost pains to aid them. In the public buildings of his town, and in other places, this client may view different woods, finish, joinery, etc., that will enable him to rightly judge of the materials and work that the contractor is giving him. There are many practical ways suggested to make him a most capable inspector.

A FACT.

We can certainly serve our clients better and at less expense than they can get elsewhere, as we have the drawings, specifications, etc., of more than one thousand building designs on file. We are familiar with the various plans and features that these designs represent, using them every day. Their reproduction economizes study, time and labor; the great saving thus effected is given to our patrons by our low charges. It is not expected that these designs will please all, but they give you ideas and suggestions and help mature your plans. Any changes can be made, enlarging, adding any new features, combining different interiors with the exteriors, etc., so as to please.

It must be evident to the owner, that building one of these designs has many advantages; he can get all the drawings, specifications, etc., promptly, and at small expense; previous contracts have confirmed our estimates; slight changes can be made without delay or affecting cost; important changes can be made promptly and the effect upon cost easily kept account of.

TO INTENDING PATRONS. BEST WAY TO PROCEED.

From the design book or books in hand, select a design and order the working plans, details, specifications, etc., from the architects, enclosing one-half of price of drawings and balance to be paid C. O. D., or send the whole price, and we will send, express charges free. The relation of client is thus established which, as with a lawyer, commands immediate advice and counsel, and subsequent watchfulness and care to the end of the case. More favorable than with lawyers, the architect's fee is definite, and with this Company very small. Upon receipt of the order, the architects will critically examine the owner's selection, with the view of giving him the benefit of any later or improved modification, if there be any. If the architects feel sure that the design selected is suitable for the client's purpose in every way and come within the cost, they will make preliminary sketches and send for correction or approval, in case any changes are desired, and do this until all is satisfactory, when they will fill the order at once and send Working Plans, Detail Drawings, Specifications, Agreements, Supplement Drawings, and Bill of Materials (the latter only when specially ordered); at the same time will be sent circulars, price lists, illustrated pamphlets, etc., of various materials and appliances. Almost everything specified for the house is described (often illustrated) and prices given. This information makes the examination of the drawings, specifications, etc., to the most inexperienced as A, B, C. He can comprehend and understand everything with a few hours study. When an owner is posted, contractors will bid lower, and for the same reason they will build better. There is never so much deception attempted upon the man who is posted. If there be anything the client does not fully understand, the architect will fully explain it, sending him more details if need be.

The most difficult part is done; the experienced owner will now know what to do; the inexperienced will be fully informed by letter or interview. By this time he will have acquired much information; many things that were strange are now plain; he has gained confidence. Our instructions about contracting, making payments, special points and matters to watch, *protection against mechanic's liens*, etc., are full and explicit, and are better conveyed in a letter to a client than printed in a book.

We instruct the client how to proceed by "day's work," if he prefers it to contracting. It is well to know, in case of unreasonable bids by contractors. Many have reason for congratulation over the result of adopting this method, particularly when they proved that the architect's estimate was ample, and that the contractors' bids were unreasonably exorbitant.

GUARANTEE.

We make this further guarantee in conclusion: If, after you have received all the plans, specifications, etc., and we have by some mistake of ours sent you the drawings for a building that you find cannot be built for the price you had limited us to or we had quoted you, we will, on their return, either change as you may desire or make you altogether new drawings free of any extra cost, and will do this until you are satisfied. This also applies to new work, if in case no design that we have can be fitted to your ideas, we will make up one to conform with same and you receive all of the above benefits. Price for new work is at the rate of $2\frac{1}{2}$ per cent. of the total cost of the building.

DESIGN No. 378.

Cost $3,300, without Plumbing, Heating or Mantels.

SECOND STORY PLAN.

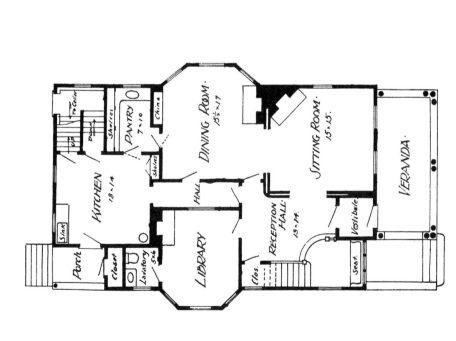

FIRST STORY PLAN.

DESCRIPTION OF DESIGN No. 378.

GENERAL DIMENSIONS.—Length, 57 ft. over veranda; width, 36 ft. Height of stories: cellar, 7 ft.; first story, 9 ft.; second story, 8 ft. 6 in.

EXTERIOR MATERIALS.—Foundation, stone; 30-inch broken ashlar above grade. Whole house sheathed with ⅞-inch matched sheathing and building paper, and covered with ½-inch lap siding on first story; second story, gables and roof covered with dipped shingles; pressed brick chimneys; paint, three coats.

INTERIOR FINISH.—Three coats of plaster, with white hard finish throughout; floor of reception hall of oak; floors of kitchen, pantry and bath room of maple; entire house finished in pine or whitewood, except reception hall, which is to be finished in oak; all finished natural or painted, as owner may desire.

ACCOMMODATIONS.—Cellar under entire house, divided by brick and wood partitions into the necessary rooms and coal bins; mantels in sitting room, dining room or library; sliding doors between reception hall and sitting room and dining room; china cabinet built in dining room; lavatory off of library; coat closet in reception hall; under main stairs; seat in reception hall on landing; rear stairs to cellar and second floor off the kitchen; closet off of rear porch; large pantry with plenty of cupboard room and a butler's sink; cupboard also off kitchen; main bedrooms have large closets; linen cupboard in bath room; good sized attic, reached by stairs from second floor hall; windows and doors all of good size and special design; front door glazed with beveled plate glass.

COST.—Contract cost, $3,300, without plumbing, heating or mantels.

Price of working drawings, specifications, etc., all in duplicate, all details and license to build, $50.00.

7

DESIGN No. 379.

Cost $7,800, without Plumbing, Heating or Mantels.

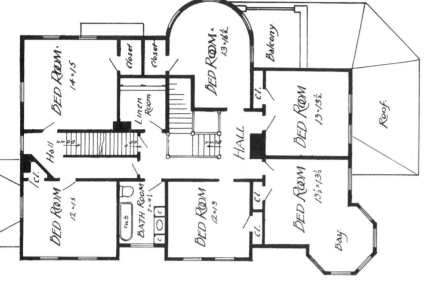

SECOND STORY PLAN.

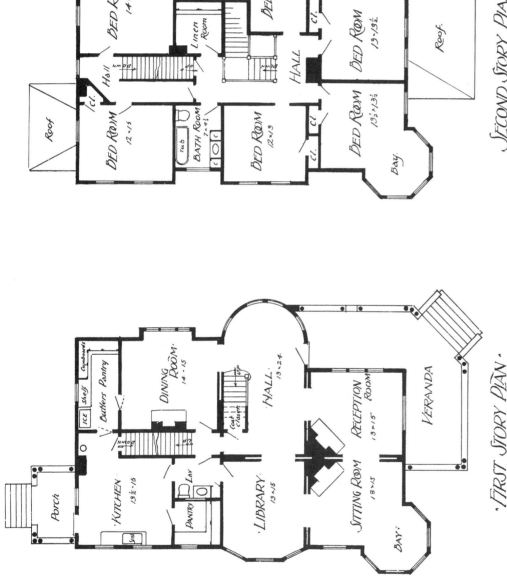

FIRST STORY PLAN.

DESCRIPTION OF DESIGN No. 379.

GENERAL DIMENSIONS.—Length, 64 ft.; width, 41 ft. Height of stories: cellar, 7 ft. 6 in.; first story, 9 ft. 6 in.; second story, 9 ft.; attic, 8 ft. 6 in.

EXTERIOR MATERIALS.—Foundation, brick; four courses of 9-inch ashlar above grade. Whole house sheathed with ⅞-inch matched sheathing and building paper, and covered with ½-inch lap siding on first story and dipped shingles on second story; dormers and roofs; chimneys of pressed brick with stone trimming; paint, three coats.

INTERIOR FINISH.—Three coats of plaster, with rough hard finish in hall, dining room, kitchen, pantry, lavatory and hall of second story; balance of plaster with white hard finish; floors of hall and dining room of quartered oak; floors of kitchen, pantry, lavatory and bath room of maple; hall and dining room finished in quartered white oak; reception room and sitting room in cherry; library in quartered sycamore; kitchen, pantry, lavatory and bath room in Georgia pine; balance of house in pine or whitewood; all finished natural in four coat work, with hard wood rubbed to a dull finish.

ACCOMMODATIONS.—Cellar under entire house, with cement floor, divided by brick division walls into the necessary rooms, such as vegetable and fruit cellars, laundry, furnace room, drying room and coal bins. Cellar ceiling plastered one coat; mantels in reception room, sitting room and dining room. Principal rooms in first story are all connected with each other by sliding doors; cove ceilings in reception room, sitting room and library; closets under main stairs; large pantry off kitchen, also butler's pantry connecting kitchen with dining room. All bed rooms have closets fitted with shelves and drawers; large linen room fitted with linen cupboard and drawers; rear stairs from cellar to kitchen, from rear hall to second story, and from second story hall to attic; two rooms finished in attic; windows and doors all of good size and special design; windows of all main rooms in first story and front bed rooms in second story glazed with plate glass; front door glazed with beveled plate glass.

COST.—Contract cost, $7,800, without plumbing, heating or mantels.

Price of working drawings, specifications, etc., all in duplicate, all details and license to build, $85.00.

DESIGN No. 489.

Contract price, $2,100, without Plumbing, Furnace or Mantels.

SECOND FLOOR PLAN

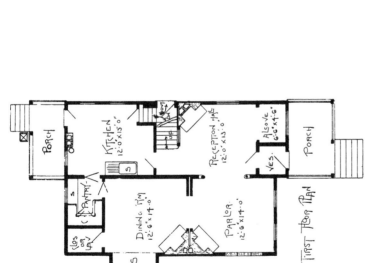

FIRST FLOOR PLAN

DESCRIPTION OF DESIGN No. 489.

GENERAL DIMENSIONS.—Width over bay, 29 ft.; length over porches, 58 ft. Height of stories: cellar, 7 ft.; first story, 9 ft. 6 in.; second story, 8 ft. 6 in.

EXTERIOR MATERIALS.—Foundation, stone; three courses of 10-inch ashlar above grade. Entire cellar cemented. Ash pits under fireplaces. Whole house sheathed with ⅞-inch matched sheathing and covered with dipped shingles as shown.

INTERIOR FINISH.—Three coats plaster and pine finish throughout. All finish detailed, doors and windows specially designed, R. H. P. & D. R., grained in imitation of quartered oak, balance of dwelling finished natural.

ACCOMMODATIONS.—Sizes of rooms, locations of closets and all fixtures as shown on plans.

COST.—Contract price, $2,100, without plumbing, furnace or mantels. Building can be erected complete for $2,400.

Price of working plans, specifications, details, etc., all in duplicate, and license to build, $40.00.

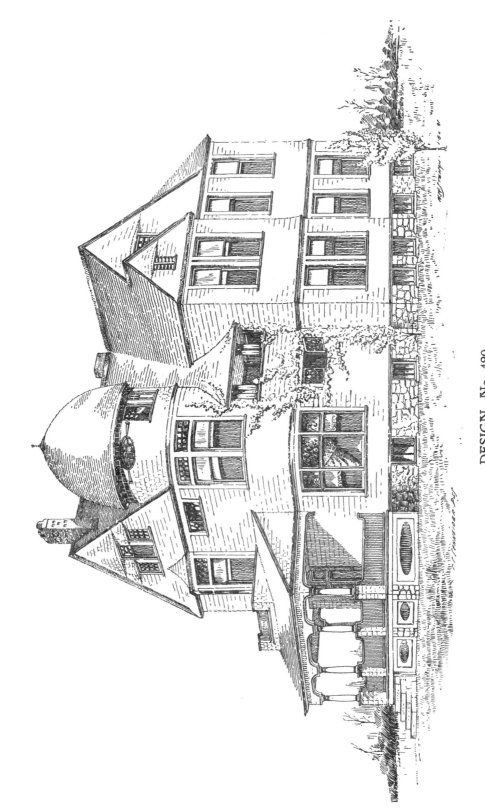

DESIGN No. 490.

Cost, $4,000 complete.

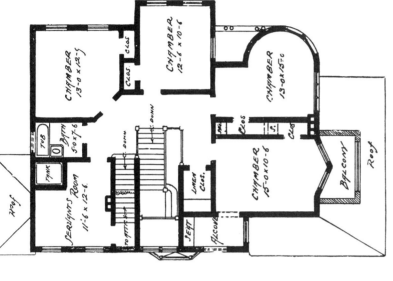

DESCRIPTION OF DESIGN No. 490.

GENERAL DIMENSIONS.—Width, 40 ft. 6 in. over bay and side entrance stoop; length, 56 ft. 6 in. over front and rear porches. Height of stories: cellar, 7 ft.; first story, 9 ft. 2 in.; second story, 8 ft. 6 in.

EXTERIOR MATERIALS.—Foundation, stone; three courses of 10-inch ashlar above grade; cellar under whole house, cemented and divided by 8-inch brick partitions into numerous rooms, such as fruit cellar, store cellar, laundry, furnace room, coal rooms, etc. Whole house sheathed with matched pine boards and building paper. First floor covered with ½-inch lap pine siding. Second floor, tower, balconies and gables shingled with California redwood shingles. Roof, black slate. Galvanized iron ridge roll.

INTERIOR FINISH.—Ceilings and walls three coats of plaster. All finish for several parts detailed in the most modern styles. The finish for the first floor to be of hard wood, as follows: parlor, cherry; reception hall, white oak; chamber, white oak; library, red oak; dining room, ash; kitchen, ash; all finished natural. Second floor finished in whitewood or pine. Doors and windows all designed. Attic floored for drying room.

ACCOMMODATIONS.—Location of rooms, closets, fixtures and sizes as shown on floor plans. This house is nicely arranged; has large, comfortable rooms with bays, arches, sliding doors and all to make a beautiful home. The attic has room enough to make good servants' chambers or dry rooms. It can be reduced in cost by reducing size, finish, etc.

COST.—This house, complete, can be built for about $4,000. This includes plumbing, furnace, mantels, painting, etc.

Price for working plans, elevations, specifications, details, etc., and license to build, $50.00.

DESIGN No. 701.

Cost, $1,900, complete.

14

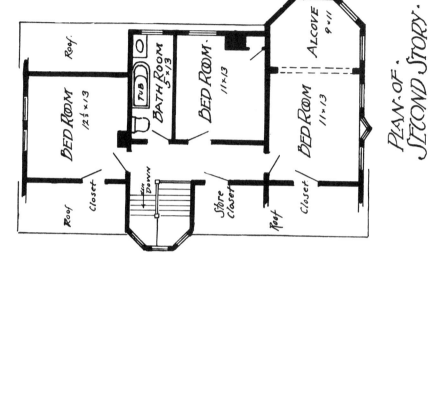

PLAN OF
SECOND STORY.

PLAN OF
FIRST STORY.

DESCRIPTION OF DESIGN No. 701.

This tasteful cottage is 29 feet in width by 43 feet in length, and has seven large rooms, exclusive of bath room and pantry. The roof and side walls are covered with dipped shingles, in harmonious colors, and the foundation is of stone, in three courses of 10-inch ashlar. A large veranda extends across the front, and an octagonal tower forms a prominent feature in the outside appearance. A neat front door opens from the veranda into a large reception room, beyond which is the wide open staircase, and at the right hand is an arched opening leading to the large living room, which has a fireplace and an alcove formed by the tower, separated from the room by an arch of fretwork. Sliding doors join the living room with the dining room, which has a door leading into the main hall. Swing doors lead through a convenient pantry to the kitchen, which has an outside door which opens on a small rear porch. The cellar stairs have an outside door on the grade level. The cellar is seven feet high and extends under the rear portion of the house, and is divided by partitions into the requisite space for coal bins and store rooms. The second story has three large bed chambers, the front room having an alcove in the tower, connected by a cased opening. Near the head of the stairs is a bath room fitted with plumbing fixtures in the open work style, and opening from the hall is a large store closet. All the bed rooms have conveniently placed closets. A pleasing feature is the staircase projection in the form of a bay with three sides, lighted at the landing by three high casement windows, set in diamond panes. The stairs are wide and of easy ascent. The entire interior is finished natural in yellow pine. The kitchen, bath room and pantry have maple floors, and are wainscoted to a height of four feet in yellow pine. The cost of erection was $1,900.

Price of working drawings, specifications, etc., all in duplicate, all details and license to build, $36.00.

15

DESIGN No. 702.

Cost, $1,600, complete.

... FIRST · FLOOR · PLAN ...

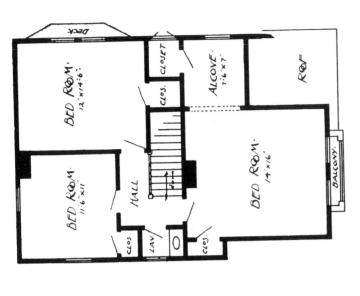

... SECOND · FLOOR · PLAN ...

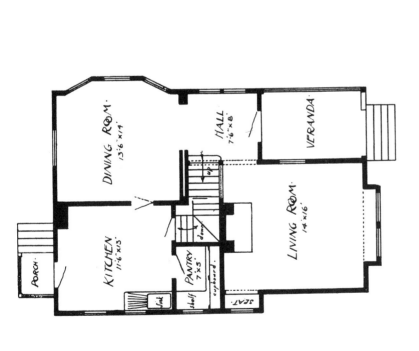

DESCRIPTION OF DESIGN No. 702.

The perspective and accompanying plans show an attractive and well arranged low cost cottage. The general dimensions are : length, 37 ft. 6 in. : width, 26 ft. 6 in.; cellar, 7 ft.; first story, 9 ft.; second story, 8 ft. 6 in. Cellar is under the rear half of building ; has cemented floor, and divided into two rooms ; furnace and coal room under dining room, and vegetable cellar under kitchen. Entrance is had from kitchen under main stairs. There is a large front porch, from which one enters a small hall, 7 ft. 6 in. by 8 ft., of ample size to be used as a reception room, and out of which the main stairs ascend. The living room and dining room are reached from this hall ; both are of good size and well lighted. Note plans as to bays, window seats, etc. A pretty piece of spindle work shows from living room on the stairway. Swinging door between dining room and kitchen. Pantry adjoining cellarway from kitchen, with large cupboards, etc. Rear entrance to dwelling from a roomy porch into kitchen. Kitchen, pantry and lavatory on second floor are floored with maple flooring and wainscoted. In the second story three large bed rooms, with plenty closets, open independently from hall. Front bed room has a pretty little alcove or dressing room to the right, with closet. There is a lavatory opposite stairway, which could be enlarged a trifle, and taking in the closet of rear bed room would give room for a folding bath tub and water closet. The attic is reached through scuttle in closet over stairs. An attic stairway could be built from this same place. The dwelling is heated by furnace and lighted by gas, also has hot and cold water plumbing to fixtures shown. The building is well built, having a stone foundation of three courses of 8-inch ashlar above grade. Walls are sheathed and covered with building paper and lap siding ; shingle roof and painted two good coats of pure lead and oil paint. Interior finish is of yellow pine throughout, finished natural. Walls plastered with white hard finish. Doors and windows all of good size and design. Cost, $1,600, complete.

Price of working drawings, specifications, etc., all in duplicate, all details and license to build, $32.00.

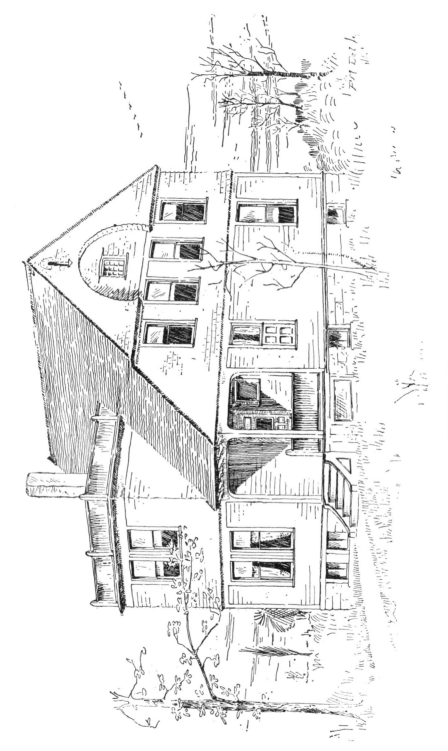

DESIGN No. 703.

Cost from $750 to $900, without Heating, Mantel or Plumbing.

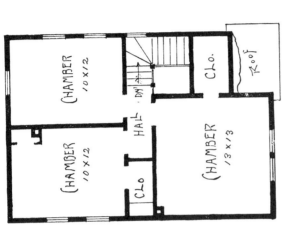

··SECOND·FLOOR··

·FIRST·FLOOR·

DESCRIPTION OF DESIGN No. 703.

GENERAL DIMENSIONS.—Length, 31 ft.; width, 21 ft. Height of stories: cellar, 6 ft. 6 in.; first story, 8 ft. 6 in.; second story, 8 ft. 4 in.

EXTERIOR MATERIALS.—Foundation, stone; three courses of 8-inch ashlar above grade. Well cellar, 12 feet in diameter, under parlor and dining room, and cemented. Whole house sheathed with Neponset building paper, and covered with ⅞-inch drop or novelty siding, first and second story different designs, and roof shingled.

INTERIOR FINISH.—Two coats of plaster, pine or whitewood finish throughout. Select stock designs for finish. All doors and windows of good size. Kitchen floored with hard pine. Open staircase.

ACCOMMODATIONS.—Sizes of all rooms, location of closets, fixtures, etc., as shown on plans. All rooms are of good size and well lighted.

COST.—Cost from $750 to $900, according to grade of stocks used.

Price of working drawings, details, specifications, etc., all in duplicate, and license to build, $21.00.

19

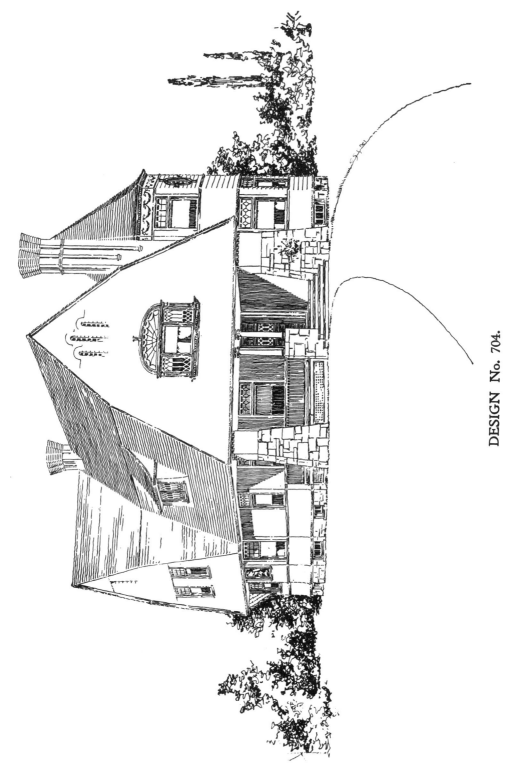

DESIGN No. 704.

Cost, $3,550, without Plumbing, Heating or Mantels.

· SECOND FLOOR PLAN ·

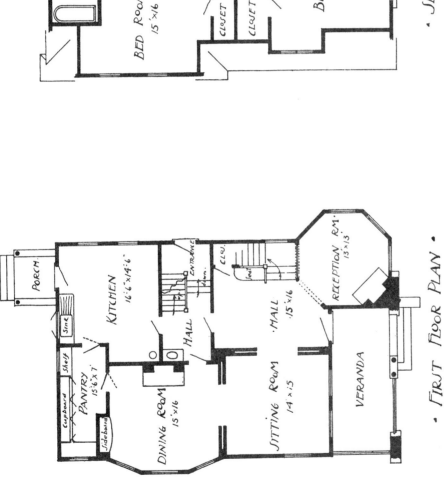

· FIRST FLOOR PLAN ·

DESCRIPTION OF DESIGN No. 704.

GENERAL DIMENSIONS.—Length, 52 ft.; width, 38 ft. Height of stories : cellar, 7 ft.; first story, 9 ft.; second story, 8 ft. 6 in.

EXTERIOR MATERIALS.—Foundation, stone; 18 inches of broken ashlar above grade; whole house sheathed on the outside with ⅞-inch matched sheathing and building paper, and covered with dipped shingles on first and second stories, gables, dormers and roofs; chimneys of pressed brick: paint, three coats.

INTERIOR FINISH.—Three coats of plaster, with rough hard finish in hall, reception room and dining room; balance of plaster with white hard finish. Floors of hall, reception room and dining room of oak; floors of kitchen, pantry, rear hall and bath room of maple; the trim in hall, reception room and sitting room to be of quartered oak; balance of house finished in pine or whitewood; all to be finished natural or painted as owner may wish.

ACCOMMODATIONS.—Cellar under entire house, divided by wood and brick partitions into the necessary rooms; mantels in reception room and dining room; sliding doors between hall and sitting room and sitting room and dining room; sideboard built in dining room; coat closet under main stairs off hall; linen closet second floor off hall; all bed rooms have large closets furnished with shelves; attic floored for light purposes, reached by scuttle in second floor hall; windows and doors all of good size and special design; front door glazed with beveled plate glass.

COST.—Contract cost, $3,550, without plumbing, heating or mantels.

Price of working drawings, specifications, etc., all in duplicate, all details and license to build, $54.00.

DESIGN No. 705.

Contract cost, $8,000, complete.

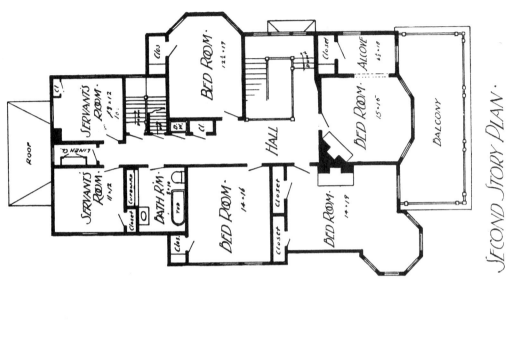

FIRST · STORY · PLAN ·

SECOND STORY PLAN ·

DESCRIPTION OF DESIGN No. 705.

The accompanying floor plans of designs shown on opposite page give a good idea of the arrangement of rooms, all of which are large and conveniently placed. The exterior is attractive and in good proportion. An octagonal tower gives boldness to the front and a wide veranda extends the whole width. The foundation has four courses of rock-faced ashlar. Numerous bays and projections lend variety to the design. The house has a width of 45 feet, and the length measures 80 feet, including the porches. The roof is of slate and the walls covered with narrow courses of lap siding. The chimneys are pressed brick. On entering the house through the vestibule, the large reception hall is reached, which, together with the vestibule, is handsomely finished in white oak, with high paneled wainscoting. To the right is a window seat with casement windows. The main stairway is somewhat elaborate in design. A carved newel post supports a handsome lamp in wrought iron. A coat closet is placed under the stairs. The drawing room, living room, dining room and library all open from the hall. The drawing room is finished in cherry, with a mantel of the same wood. The living room, which is connected with the living room by sliding doors, is finished in quartered oak, with floor of the same material, having a parquet border. This room is wainscoted in oak, and has a handsome sideboard. A curved bay with four large windows affords light, and on either side are niches for china, which have glass doors of ornamental pattern. The library has a wide bay window, affording ample light and adjoining is a small lavatory and also a closet. This room is finished in quartered sycamore. From the main hall opens a door leading to the rear or servant's hall, from which rise the rear stairs, and a flight of steps lead to the cellar. The culinary department of the house is well arranged and convenient. The cook's pantry and the butler's pantry are both large and well lighted, and are connected by an opening and sliding door. Both are provided with sinks. The kitchen and pantries are finished in yellow pine, and have maple floors. The second story has six large bed rooms, each of which has one or more closets, and there is also a bath room and linen closet. The two front bed rooms have mantels. All rooms on this floor are finished in yellow pine. The billiard room is lighted by dormers in the roof, and is finished in yellow pine. There is a large store room and a billiard room, which has an alcove in the tower. The fixtures in the bath room are of open work pattern. The third floor has two servant's bed rooms. A dumb waiter operates from this floor to the basement. In the latter are numerous rooms separated by brick walls. The laundry is fitted with wash trays of the most approved pattern and a slop sink. There is a vegetable cellar with large hanging shelf, and also two large store rooms, adjoining which is a small wine cellar under the tower. The furnace occupies a central position, with a cold air room and ample coal bins adjoining. The entire basement has a cement floor, and the walls are brick, the exterior walls being faced with stone ashlar. The cost of this residence was about $8,000.

COST.—Contract cost, $8,000, complete.

Price of working drawings, specifications, etc., all in duplicate, all details and license to build, $100.00.

23

DESIGN No. 706.

Cost, $3,600, complete.

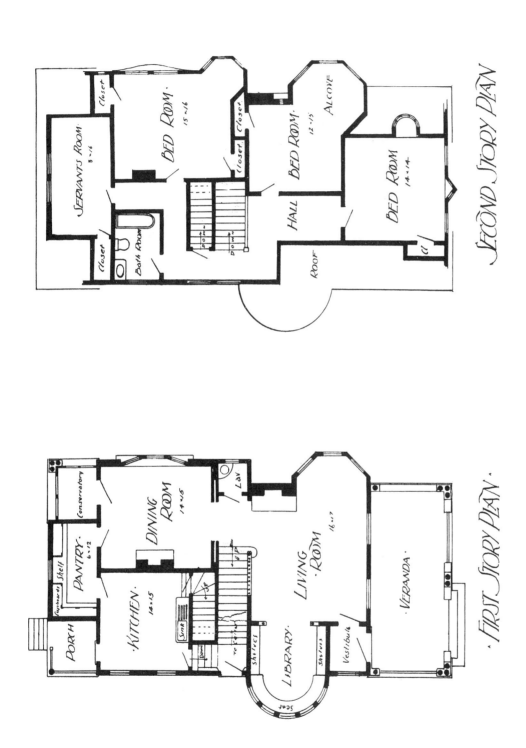

FIRST STORY PLAN

SECOND STORY PLAN

DESCRIPTION OF DESIGN No. 706.

The perspective and plans illustrated present a very artistic treatment of the exterior, and possess at the same time the merit of being convenient with regard to inside arrangements and details. This residence can be constructed at a cost of about $3,600, although this fixture would be affected by style of finish. The length is 56 feet, including porch; width, 32 feet. Height of stories: first story, 10 feet; second story, 9 feet. Under the entire house should be a basement having a height of seven feet with cemented floor. This cellar can be divided by brick or wood partitions into laundry, vegetable cellar, furnace room and fuel basement. Over matched sheathing and Neponset building paper are dipped shingles. The roof is to be shingled, but dipped in a contrasting color by which the outward appearance is enhanced. The entire house is placed on a stone foundation, which may be of three courses of ashlar above grade. The chimneys being of stone and in irregular courses, add to the general effect which is heightened by the octagonal tower rising above the roof. Below the tower, as shown in the plans, the octagon bay forms an alcove in the bed room up stairs, and a bay window to the living room down stairs. A spacious veranda occupies the entire front of the house. The vestibule which connects the veranda with the living room is placed with regards to its convenience, without forming unnecessary angles. The living room is large and well lighted, while the unique disposition of the library is at once apparent. The circular bay in the library is well supplied with windows, and upon the inside an oak seat is fitted to its entire length, from each end of which extend the shelving or book cases. The library and living rooms are to be connected with an ornamental arch, in which columns and grille work may be placed to improve the decorative detail. The stairs are wide and ascend from the rear of the living room. Opposite the stairs is the lavatory. Convenience is studied in the servant's stairs leading from the kitchen to the second floor and separated from the main stairway by a partition. Back of the dining room is the conservatory, and entrance is also had to the kitchen through the pantry. Up stairs the arrangement is complete. The front bed room is supplied with an extending oriel window at the front and a dormer window at the side. The hall extends from the front bed room around the stairways to the servant's room; bath room to be supplied complete with open plumbing work; all bed rooms have ample closets. The living room, library and vestibule are to be finished in oak; the dining room in sycamore, while the kitchen and pantry are in Georgia pine, all finished natural. Floors of all rooms should be hard wood, natural finish; up stairs finish to be in Norway pine, natural. Mantels and open grates ornament the living room and dining room. Building heated by furnace.

Price of working drawings, specifications, etc., all in duplicate, all details and license to build, $54.00.

DESIGN No. 707.

Contract cost, $2,300, complete.

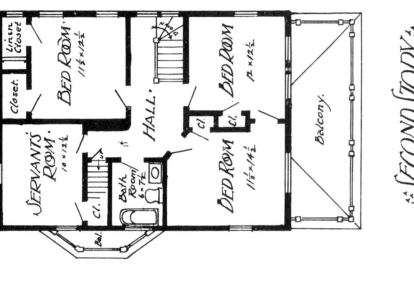

SECOND STORY.

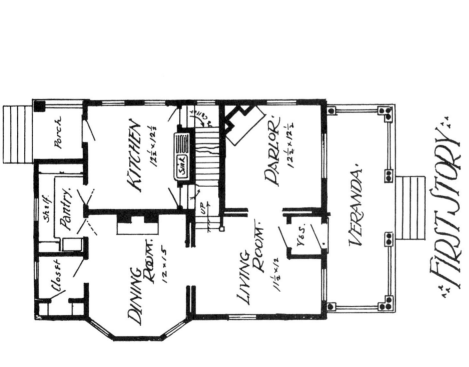

FIRST STORY.

DESCRIPTION OF DESIGN No. 707.

The perspective and floor plans given show a popular style of frame residence. The exterior appearance is very pleasing and the interior arrangement contains both comfort and convenience. The build'g is 29 by 44 feet in size, and location of closets and fixtures as shown on the plans. The foundation is of blue sandstone, cellar cemented throughout under the whole building, divided into different rooms, such as coal room, vegetable and fruit cellar and laundry. The first story is of narrow lapped siding, second story and roofs of dipped cedar shingles. The living room is entered from the vestibule, which has a parquet floor. Parlor, living room and dining room are finished in quartered white oak, also the first run of stairs leading out of the living room. The remainder of the building is finished in yellow pine. Kitchen, pantry, bath room and cellarway are wainscoted four feet high. Sliding doors, as shown, between the living room and parlor and living room and dining room. Swinging doors lead to the pantry and kitchen. Brick mantel and fireplace is placed in the dining room, and gas grate and mantel in the parlor. The combination entrance is shown to main stairway from the kitchen. In the second story are four large bed rooms with ample closets. Bath room, off the main hall, is fitted out with hot and cold water and open plumbing. The house is heated by hot air furnace in the basement and lighted by gas.

Price of working drawings, specifications, etc., all in duplicate, all details and license to build, $40.00.

DESIGN No. 708.

Cost, **$12,500**, complete.   Many changes can be made to lessen expense.

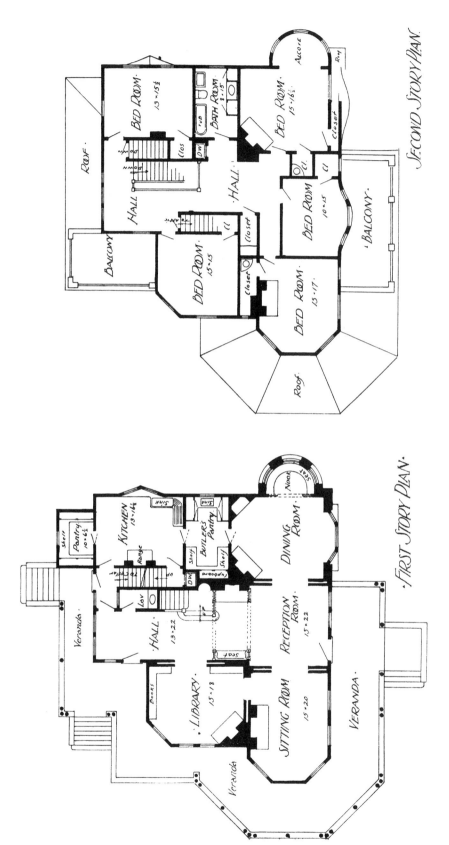

SECOND STORY PLAN.

FIRST STORY PLAN.

DESCRIPTION OF DESIGN No. 708.

With a view to illustrating a design of a dwelling that may be erected to advantage where abundance of land may be had, we give this one, embodying a number of novel features. The exterior is to be of stone and frame first story and balance of shingle work. The color of the roof to be such as to contrast harmoniously with that of the sides, while by further trimming a handsome effect is produced. A foundation of stone supports the structure. Stone is to be used also in the construction of the veranda, a portion of the first story and the chimneys. The spacious veranda extends around the house on three sides and is reached by three flights of stone steps placed at front, side and rear, respectively. The plan is noteworthy for convenience of arrangement and ready accessibility of the various rooms. Dimensions in general are as follows : width, exclusive of veranda, 62 feet ; length (depth), 56 feet. Veranda has an average width of ten feet. Height of stories : cellar, 7½ feet ; first story, 10 feet ; second story, 9 feet. Cellar to be under entire house, cemented and divided into furnace and coal rooms, vegetable cellar, laundry and storage room as desired. The four main rooms of the first floor are thrown together by archways provided with sliding doors. A wide hall extends through the center of the house, the front portion of which, by a unique arrangement of the archways of columns and grille work, is made the reception room. Back of the reception room and within the two archways composed of columns, spindle base and overhead grille work, is formed a nook containing at one end a polished oak seat, and on the opposite side an ornamental mantel and open grate. Immediately after this nook is located the wide stairway, a turn being made at the third step, under which is placed a lavatory. A pleasing feature of the dining room is that it is located in the front of the house. It is also supplied with a nook having oak seat and separated by drapery. Between the dining room and kitchen is the butler's pantry supplied with all conveniences. The kitchen is of good size, back of which is the cook's pantry. The servants' stairway is reached from the kitchen. A dumb waiter operates from cellar to attic. Beside the hall nook, the sitting room, dining room and library are to contain mantels of artistic pattern and open grates. On the second floor five large bed rooms, with generous closets, and bath room are located, all easy accessible from the wide hall. The two larger front bed rooms are embellished with mantels of tasteful designs, and possess the additional convenience of closets containing stationary bowls. All plumbing is complete and of the open work. A roomy attic is reached by stairs leading up from the rear hall on the second floor. Interior finish of building is to be of quartered white oak, select cherry, quartered sycamore and bird's eye maple, all finished natural except kitchen and second story, which should be Norway pine. Floors on first story hard wood, kitchen and pantries being maple. The three front rooms may be treated with parquetry borders to great benefit. The cost of this structure is estimated at $12,500, which may be modified in proportion to style of finish.

Price of working drawings, specifications, etc., all in duplicate, all details and license to build, $150.00.

DESIGN No. 709.

Cost, $2,500, complete.

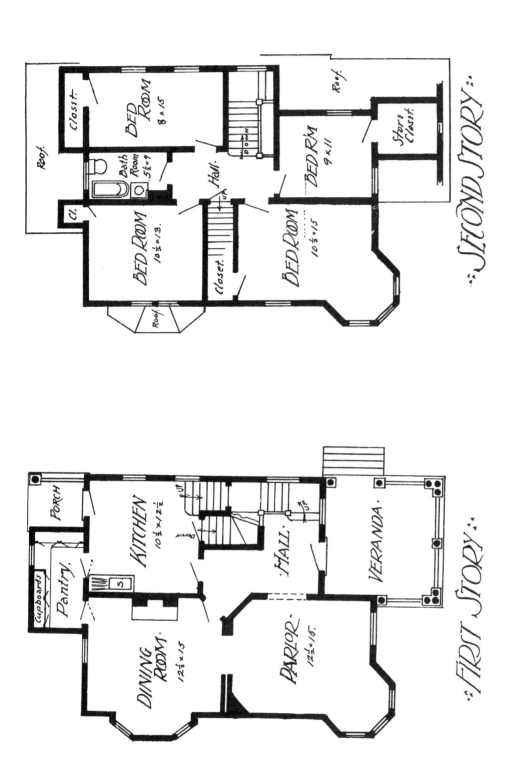

: FIRST STORY :

: SECOND STORY :

DESCRIPTION OF DESIGN No. 709.

This cottage is 29 feet wide by 46 feet in length over veranda and pantry. Same has seven large rooms without the reception hall, bath room and pantry; cellar is under the whole building, 7 feet in height and cemented throughout and divided into necessary rooms by partitions. Foundation is of stone, three courses of 10-inch ashlar; building is sheathed on the outside and covered on the first story with narrow lap siding, second story and roofs with dipped shingles; doors and windows all of good size and design, making the building well lighted; sliding door between dining room and parlor; swinging doors leading into the pantry from both dining room and kitchen. There is a combination stairway from front hall and kitchen, leading to the second story. Bay windows in the dining room and parlor. Octagon bay in parlor is extended to the second story, forming a tower. The building is finished throughout in yellow pine, with hardwood floors in hall, dining room, kitchen, pantry and bath room, the latter three being wainscoted in narrow beaded ceiling four feet high. A brick fireplace is shown in dining room. Bath room leading to a hall in the rear part of the second story, has all the necessary fixtures, fitted for hot and cold water. The house is heated by a hot air furnace in the basement; laundry fitted up with wash trays and slop sink. The complete cost of this building is $2,500, and same has been erected for about $2,000.

Price of working drawings, specifications, etc., all in duplicate, all details and license to build, $40.00.

DESIGN No. 710.

Cost, $2,500, complete.

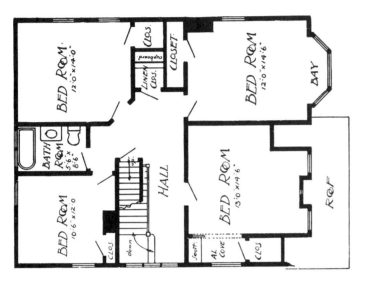

· FIRST FLOOR PLAN ·

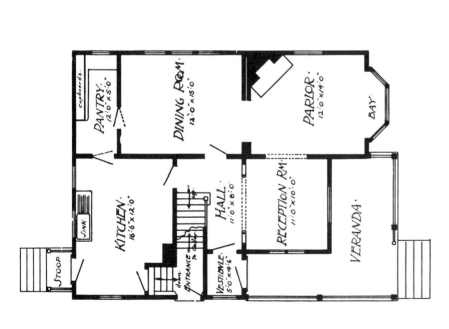

· SECOND FLOOR PLAN ·

DESCRIPTION OF DESIGN No. 710.

GENERAL DIMENSIONS.—Length, 40 ft. over front porch; width, 30 ft. Height of stories: cellar, 7 ft.; first floor, 9 ft. 2 in.; second floor, 8 ft. 6 in.

EXTERIOR MATERIALS.—Foundation, stone; three courses of 10-inch ashlar above grade. First story, lap siding; second story, gables, dormers and roof covered with dipped shingles. Paint, three coats.

INTERIOR FINISH.—Three coats of plaster, white hard finish throughout. Floors of vestibule, hall, reception room and dining room of quartered white oak with border; in kitchen, pantry and bath room of maple; balance of floors of white pine. Finish in vestibule, hall, staircase, reception room and dining room of quartered white oak. Parlor of quartered select sycamore. Finish throughout balance of dwelling is of select yellow pine. All the work is of special design; all pine finished natural in three coat work and left in the gloss. All other finish in oak and sycamore including oak floors finished natural in four coat work and rubbed to a dull finish.

ACCOMMODATIONS.—Cellar under entire building, with cemented floor. Necessary rooms, such as vegetable cellar, laundry and coal bins divided off by wood partitions. Building sheathed on the outside with ⅞-inch matched sheathing and covered with Neponset building paper. Sliding doors between dining room and parlor. Fire place in parlor with ash pit in cellar. Pantry is amply fitted out with cupboards, drawers, flour bin, etc. Good closets off all bed rooms. Linen closet fitted with drawers and cupboards. Bath room has all the fixtures and supplied with hot and cold water. Closet and wash trays in laundry. Attic floored throughout. Windows and doors all of good size and design.

CONTRACT COST.—$2,500 complete. Price of working drawings, all details, specifications, etc., all in duplicate, and license to build, $45.00.

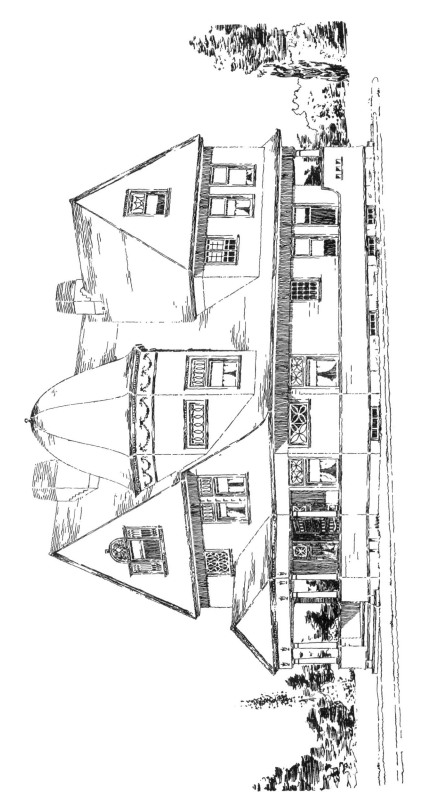

DESIGN No. 711.

Contract cost, $2,500.

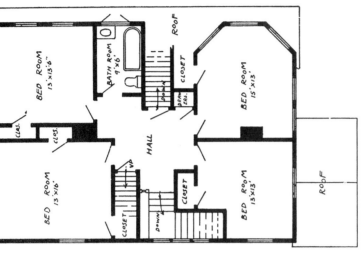

▲ SECOND FLOOR PLAN ▲

▲ FIRST FLOOR PLAN ▲

DESCRIPTION OF DESIGN No. 711.

GENERAL DIMENSIONS.—Length, 49 ft. 6 in. over veranda ; width, 29 ft. 6 in. Height of stories : cellar, 7 ft.; first floor, 9 ft.; second story, 8 ft. 6 in.

EXTERIOR MATERIALS.—Foundation, stone, one course of 14-inch ashlar above grade. First story, lap siding ; second story, gables, roof, dormers, dipped shingles. Chimneys, pressed brick. Paint, three coats.

INTERIOR FINISH.—Three coats of plaster, rough hard finish in reception hall, lavatory, dining room, second floor hall and bath room. White hard finish in balance of house. Floors of reception hall and lavatory, oak ; floors of kitchen, pantry and bath room, maple ; floors of balance of house hard pine. Finish is all to be of selected white pine or poplar, except in reception hall, including staircase, same to be of oak. All finish is to be of special design, finished natural. Hardwood finished natural.

ACCOMMODATIONS.—Cellar under entire house with cemented floor, divided by wood partitions into the necessary rooms and coal pins. House sheathed on the outside with ⅞-inch matched sheathing. Sliding doors between reception hall and dining room. Fireplaces in reception hall and dining room. Conservatory off dining room ; lavatory off reception hall. Butler's pantry has plenty of cupboard room, and is also furnished with drawers and flour bin. Rear stairs to second floor, accessible from reception hall and kitchen. Case of drawers for linen on second floor. Good closet room off all bed rooms. Attic floored, but not finished, reached by stairs from second floor hall. Windows and doors of good size and design.

COST.—Contract cost, $2,500, complete. Price of working drawings, all details, specifications, etc., all in duplicate and license to build, $42.00.

DESIGN No. 712.

Contract cost, $3,200.

SECOND FLOOR PLAN.

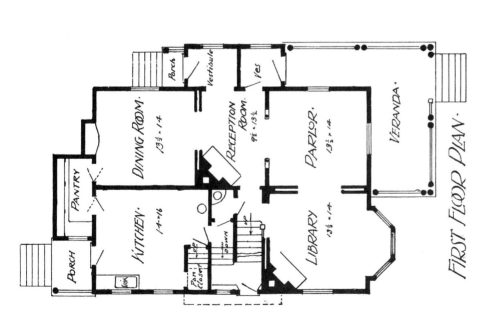

FIRST FLOOR PLAN.

DESCRIPTION OF DESIGN No. 712.

GENERAL DIMENSIONS.—Length, 55 ft.; width, 35 ft. Height of stories: cellar, 7 ft.; first story, 9 ft.; second story, 8 ft. 6 in.

EXTERIOR MATERIALS.—Foundation, stone, four courses of 9-inch ashlar above grade. Whole house sheathed with ⅞-inch matched sheathing and building paper, and covered with ½-inch lap siding on first story and dipped shingles on second story, gables, dormers and roof; pressed brick chimneys; paint, three coats.

INTERIOR FINISH.—Three coats of plaster, with white hard finish throughout; cove ceilings in parlor, library, reception room and dining room. Oak flooring in vestibule, reception room, dining room and hall. Maple floors in kitchen, pantry, lavatory and bath room. Entire house finished in white pine or whitewood finished natural or painted to suit owner.

ACCOMMODATIONS.—Cellar under entire house, with cement floor, divided by brick and wood partitions into the necessary rooms. Sliding doors between library and parlor, library and hall, reception room and dining room, and two front bed rooms; bay windows in library and one bed room; mantels in library and reception room; sideboard built in dining room. Lavatory off hall and kitchen; pan closet off kitchen; special design arch between reception room and parlor; large linen room off second floor hall. All bed rooms have good sized closets. Windows and doors all of good size and special design. Front door glazed with plate glass.

CONTRACT COST.—$3,200, complete. Price of working drawings, specifications, etc., all in duplicate, all details and license to build, $50.00.

DESIGN No. 713.

Cost, $3,700, complete.

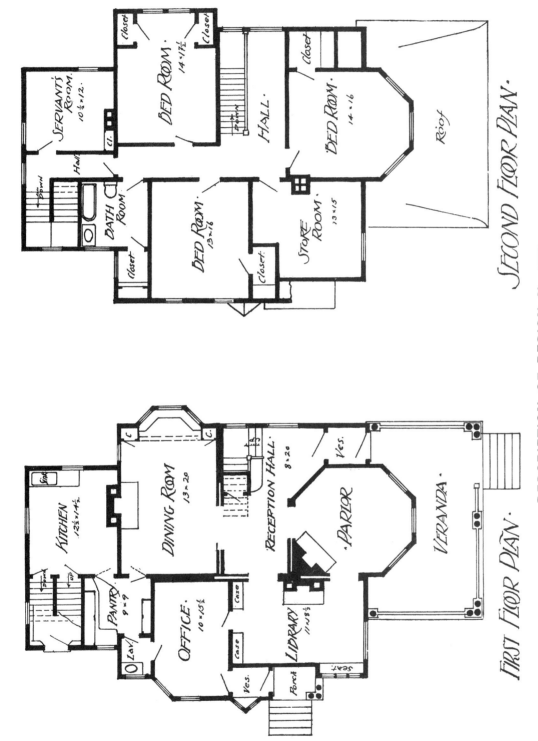

FIRST FLOOR PLAN.

SECOND FLOOR PLAN.

DESCRIPTION OF DESIGN No. 713.

GENERAL DIMENSIONS.—Length, 62 ft. over porch; width, 40 ft. over bays. Height of stories: cellar, 7 ft.; first story, 9 ft.; second, 8 ft. 6 in.

EXTERIOR MATERIALS.—Foundation, stone; three courses of 10-inch ashlar as shown. Whole house sheathed with ⅞-inch matched sheathing and building paper, and covered with ½-inch lap pine siding and black slate roof; pressed brick chimneys; paint, three coats.

INTERIOR FINISH.—Three coats of plaster, rough hard finish in vestibule, reception hall, upper hall and dining room, with cove ceilings; balance of house with white hard finish. Floors of quartered white oak; reception hall and dining room to be of quartered oak with parquet border. Reception hall stairs and dining room finished in select quartered white oak; parlor finished in select quartered sycamore; all other rooms, etc., finished in yellow pine, excepting front bedroom in second story, which is finished in whitewood with enamel colors. All finish is to be especially detailed. All hardwood and front bedroom finished in four coat work, rubbed to a dull finish. Hardwood floors finished natural and waxed.

ACCOMMODATIONS.—Cellar under entire house, with cement floor, divided by brick division walls into the necessary rooms, such as vegetable and fruit cellars, laundry, furnace room and coal bins. Cellar ceiling plastered one coat. China closet and window seat built in dining room. Window seat and book cases built in library. Sliding doors between library and parlor, library and reception hall, reception hall and parlor, and reception hall and dining room as shown. Fireplaces in parlor, library and dining room. Paneled wainscoting in vestibules, reception hall and dining room, and chair rail in office. Picture mould throughout all rooms. All bedrooms have closets as shown; coat room under main stairs. Combination outside cellar and kitchen the building. Linen cupboard in bath room. Bath room in second story; lavatory in first story, off from the office, with hot and cold water throughout entrance, also rear stairs to second story, leading from kitchen. Small attic reached by scuttle in rear hall. Windows and doors all of good size and special design. Library, parlor, reception hall and front bedroom glazed with American plate glass. Special windows as shown, glazed with leaded glass of special design. Front, side and vestibule doors of quartered white oak, glazed with American plate glass.

COST.—Contract cost, $3,700, complete. Price of working drawings, specifications, etc., all in duplicate, all details and license to build, $60.00.

DESIGN No. 714.

Cost, from $6,500 to $7,000 complete.

W.M.Hall
Del.

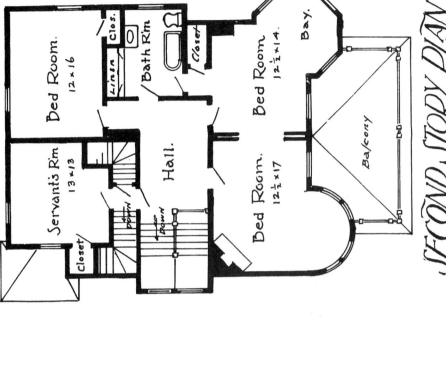

SECOND STORY PLAN

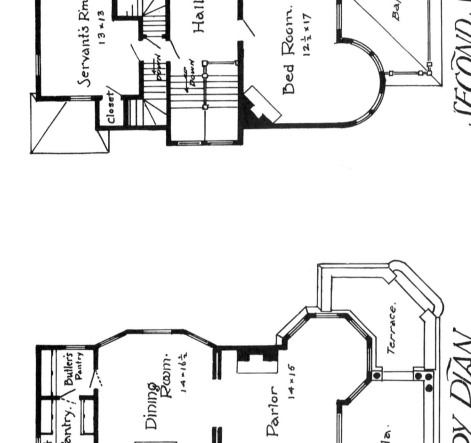

FIRST STORY PLAN

DESCRIPTION OF DESIGN No. 714.

Accompanying floor plans give a good idea of the arrangement of all rooms, which are of good size. The exterior is not purely Colonial, but is attractive in design and in good proportion. An octagon tower starts from the basement, giving beautiful bays in parlor and bedroom on the first and second floors. A round bay forms an alcove on the other side of the building and balances the front in good proportion. The foundation is of blue Amherst stone, basement under the whole building, divided into the following rooms by brick partitions: Coal room, fruit and vegetable and store cellar and laundry, which is fitted with wash trays, hot and cold water throughout, and water closet in the same. The rest of the building is of frame, roof is of small red slate, side walls are covered with narrow lap siding, belt courses, etc., as are shown on the elevations. The house is well sheathed. The chimneys are of cream colored pressed brick. Entrance to veranda is made through open terrace, all cemet floor and stone steps leading to the same. The reception room is entered through the vestibule, with marble wainscoting and tiled floor. The front door is a large massive oak door, with oval beveled plate glass. Reception room, alcove and main stairway are finished in select quartered white oak, parlor in dark mahogany, dining room in white mahogany, and two main bedrooms on second floor in cherry; bath room, rear bedrooms and all other parts on the first and second floors in select red oak. There are parquet floors in dining room, reception room and alcove. Select white maple floors in the kitchen, pantry, butler's pantry, and bath room, the floor in the latter having a parquet borders. Mantel and fireplace in reception room are constructed of light cream colored brick and terra cotta work. Mantels in other rooms are specially detailed and finished the same as the finish in the respective rooms. The windows are of plate glass throughout. Doors are all veneered the same as the finish in the respective rooms. All work is nicely detailed, and special features are introduced in the way of archways, stair work, china closet in dining room, linen closet in bath room, etc. The work is carried out in the very best manner possible. The building is plastered throughout with King's Windsor Cement Plaster, cove ceilings in the parlor and dining room, with plaster cornice, all especially detailed, and ceiling in reception hall beamed in oak. There is an outside combination entrance leading directly into the basement or to the first floor. The front and rear staircase, as shown on the plans. By noting plans one can see that the servants' part of the house can be shut off from the other part, as the rear stairs land in a passage way between the upper hall and the servants' room. The stairs to the attic also starting from this point. The bath room is well fitted with modern fixtures. Hot and cold water throughout the building. Toilet arrangements on every floor. The building is heated throughout by the hot water system and lighted by gas. The sizes of rooms and location of closets and fixtures may be seen by referring to the plans. The building is erected with the idea of having all modern improvements of every kind and description; no expense is to be spared in this modern dwelling. The attic is all finished throughout, having ample room for billiard parlor, etc. Cellar ceiling is plastered throughout.

The cost of this residence complete is about $6,500 to $7,000. Price of working drawings, specifications, etc., all in duplicate, all details and license to build, $75.00.

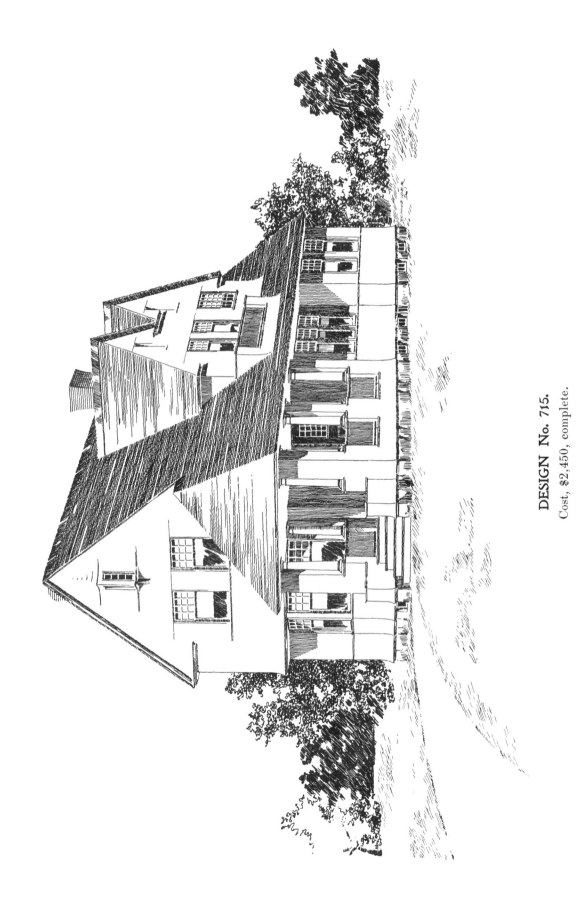

DESIGN No. 715.

Cost, $2,450, complete.

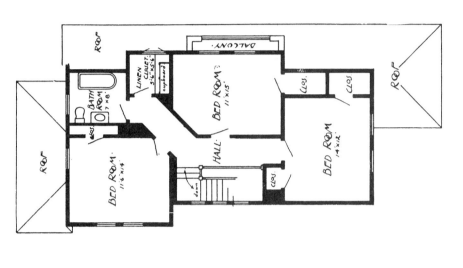

··· FIRST · FLOOR · PLAN ···

··· SECOND · FLOOR · PLAN ···

DESCRIPTION OF DESIGN No. 715.

This style of cottage has been very popular on lots from 35 feet in width and over, allowing ample room for driveway. The construction is such as to produce a warm building in winter and an exceptionally agreeable one in summer, having large veranda and rooms so arranged as to be easily ventilated. The building is 49 feet in length and 26 feet in width. Cellar under reception hall, kitchen and dining room, seven feet in depth, and divided into three rooms, furnace and coal room under reception hall, and either one or other of two remaining rooms to be used for laundry in one and vegetable cellar in other. First story is nine feet in height, and second story eight feet six inches. Entrance from veranda is had through a good sized vestibule into reception hall, from which the main stairs lead to second story. A pretty seat is built between first run of stairs, and a convenient coat closet to the right. Sitting room or parlor can be closed off from reception hall by a large sliding door. This room has a pretty bay and also fireplace and mantel. The dining room to the rear of the reception hall can be closed off by a pair of sliding doors, and also has a pretty fireplace and mantel of brick and terra cotta work. This is a very pretty room and of good size, convenient to pantry, and has, like the reception hall, an oak floor. The pantry is very large and has plenty of cupboards, etc., located in the rear of the kitchen and dining room with double swinging doors into both. Kitchen is of a very nice size and has sink. Cellar entrance well located, and rear entrance to kitchen is from a large porch. Kitchen, pantry and bathroom are all wainscoted and have maple floors. All other floors not mentioned are of soft pine. Bathroom, three large bedrooms and linen closet have entrance from upper hall. Plenty of closets throughout. Bathroom has all fixtures and hot and cold water. Building lighted by gas and heated by furnace. The foundation is of stone, one course of 12-inch ashlar shown above grade. Building is sheathed with ⅞-inch matched sheathing and building paper and covered on side walls with lap-siding, and has a dipped shingle roof. Painted in colors to suit the owner, three coats of lead and oil paint. Inside is finished in either pine, whitewood or yellow pine, tinted or finished natural as directed. Plastered walls, three coats, with white hard finish. Cove ceilings in sitting room, reception hall and dining room. Front and vestibule doors of oak and windows of good size and glazed with beveled plate glass. All other doors and windows of good size and design.

Cost, $2,450 complete. Price of working drawings, specifications, etc., all in duplicate, all details and license to build, $40.00.

DESIGN No. 716.

Contract cost, $2,250.

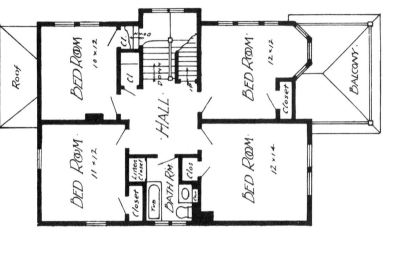

SECOND STORY

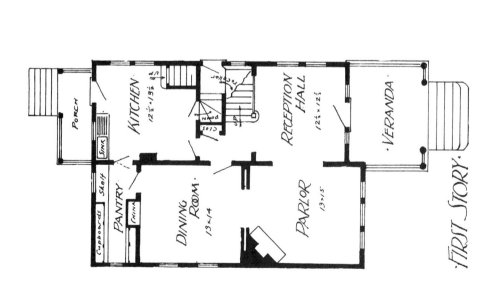

FIRST STORY.

DESCRIPTION OF DESIGN No. 716.

The length is 44 feet, inclusive of porch, and the width 26 feet 6 inches. The height of stories are: basement, 7 feet; first story 9 feet, and second story 8 feet 4 inches. Over the second story is a spacious attic, well lighted by dormer windows, and a gable which covers the attic stairs. A servants' bedroom occupies a portion of the attic. The roof is covered with slate, and the side walls are a combination of shingles and narrow siding. The foundation is of stone in courses of rock-faced ashlar, the chimneys being brick, with plain stone caps. The front porch, 10 feet in width, has a balcony over, with neat posts and railing; the front door is of oak, glazed with plate glass set in copper, and on either side of the door are windows glazed in the same style. A reception hall opens directly from the veranda, and beyond are seen the stairs, with newel post and railing of a pleasing design. An arch opening opens into the parlor, while sliding doors connect with the dining room beyond. These three rooms have coved ceilings, and all are finished in Norway pine. The parlor has a corner fireplace; the kitchen has an outside door opening on a rear porch, while doors from the same room lead to the rear stairs, to second floor and to the basement stairs, which are provided with an outside door at the grade level. The pantry is fitted completely with cupboards, shelves and drawers, and has two windows. In the second story the central portion of the house is occupied by the hall and bath room, together with a linen closet. Four large chambers, each with a good closet, take up the remaining space. Stairs to the attic lead upward from the hall. The house is heated by a furnace and is furnished with hot and cold water plumbing. The basement has a room for laundry, fitted up with wash trays and slop sink. There is a water closet in the basement. This house was erected at a cost of $2,250.

Cost.—Contract cost, $2,250, complete. Price of working drawings, specifications, etc., all in duplicate, all details and license to build, $36.00.

45

DESIGN No. 717.
Contract cost, $3,500.

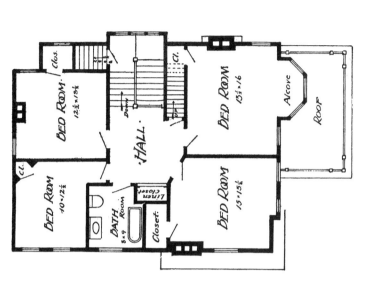

SECOND FLOOR PLAN·

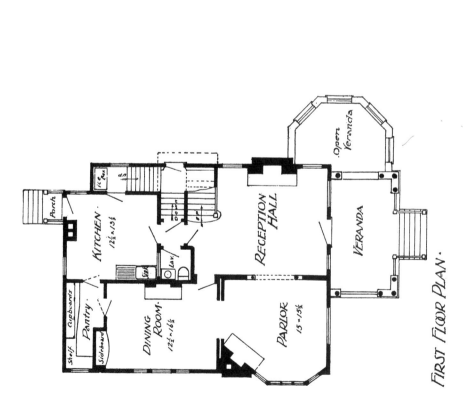

FIRST FLOOR PLAN·

DESCRIPTION OF DESIGN No. 717.

GENERAL DIMENSIONS.—Length, 50 ft. over front porch; width 34 ft. Height of stories: cellar, 7 ft.; first story, 9 ft. 6 in.; second story, 9 ft.

EXTERIOR MATERIALS.—Foundation, brick, four courses of 9-inch ashlar above grade. Whole house sheathed with ⅞-inch matched sheathing and building paper, and covered with ½-inch lap siding on first story, and dipped shingles on second story, gables and roof; chimneys of pressed brick; paint, three coats.

INTERIOR FINISH.—Three coats of plaster, with rough hard finish in reception hall, dining room and hall of second story; balance of house with white hard finish. Floors of reception hall and dining room to be of quartered white oak with parquet border; floors of pantry, kitchen, lavatory and bath room, maple; reception hall and dining room finished in quartered white oak; parlor finished in cherry; balance of house finished in white pine or whitewood. All finished natural or painted to suit owner.

ACCOMMODATIONS.—Cellar under entire house, with cement floor, divided by brick and wood division walls into the necessary rooms, such as vegetable and fruit cellars, laundry, furnace room and coal bins. Mantels in reception hall, parlor and dining room; mantel in dining room fitted with gas log. Sliding doors between parlor and dining room; special design opening between reception hall and parlor; sideboard built in dining room; linen cupboard off hall on second floor. All bed rooms have good sized closets, furnished with shelves and drawers. Good sized attic, reached by stairs from second floor hall. Windows and doors all of good size and special design; windows of reception hall, dining room and two front bedrooms glazed with plate glass; front door glazed with beveled plate glass.

COST.—Contract cost, $3,500, complete. Price of working drawings, specifications, etc., all in duplicate all details and license to build, $55.00.

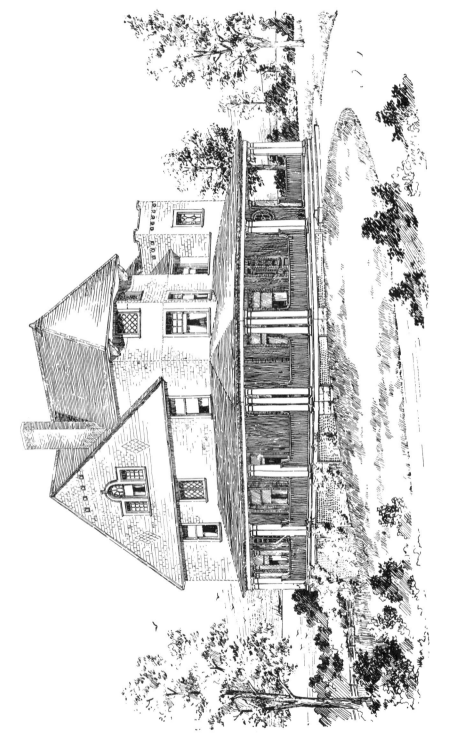

DESIGN No. 718.

Contract cost, $2,800.

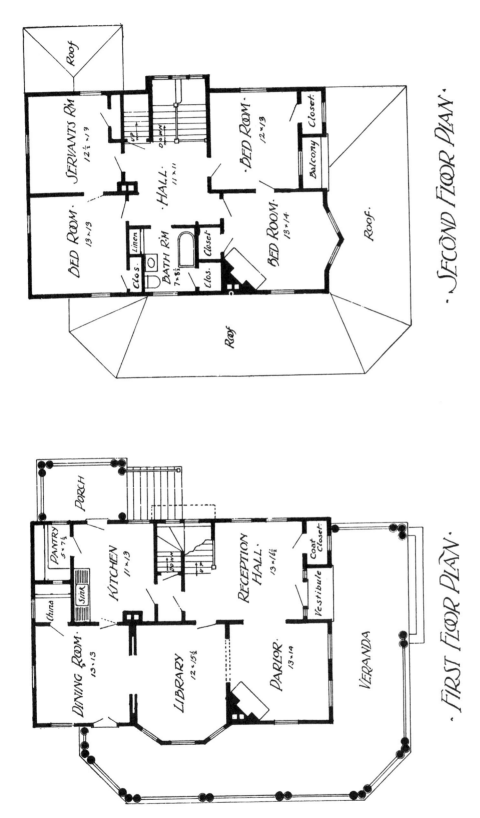

· SECOND FLOOR PLAN ·

· FIRST FLOOR PLAN ·

DESCRIPTION OF DESIGN No. 718.

GENERAL DIMENSIONS.—Length, 52 ft. over porch; width, 46 ft. over porch. Height of stories: cellar, 7 ft. 6 in.; first story, 9 ft.; second story, 8 ft. 6 in.

EXTERIOR MATERIALS.—Foundation, stone; ashlar in 12-inch courses as shown. Whole house sheathed with ⅞-inch matched sheathing and building paper, and covered with lap siding, first story; second story and gables, shingles; shingle roof; pressed brick chimneys; paint, two coats; all shingles dipped.

INTERIOR FINISH.—Three coats of plaster, with white hard finish throughout. Floors of reception hall and dining room to be of quartered oak and parquet border. China closet, pantry and bath room have maple floors, balance of house floored with soft pine. Finish is all to be of select pine or whitewood, especially detailed, and finished natural in three coat work. Hardwood floors finished natural.

ACCOMMODATIONS.—Cellar under entire house, with cement floor divided into the necessary rooms, such as vegetable and fruit cellar, laundry and furnace room. Sliding doors between dining room and library. Fireplace in parlor and front bed room. Bath room in second story. Linen cupboard in bath room. Hot and cold water throughout. All bed rooms have closets, also coat room off reception hall. Balcony over porch, reached from front bed room. Attic floored throughout, reached by stairs. Windows and doors all of good size and design. Front door of quartered oak glazed with beveled American plate glass.

COST.—Contract cost, $2,800, complete. Price of working drawings, specifications, etc., all in duplicate, all details and license to build, $45.00.

DESIGN No. 719.

Contract cost, $2,300.

50

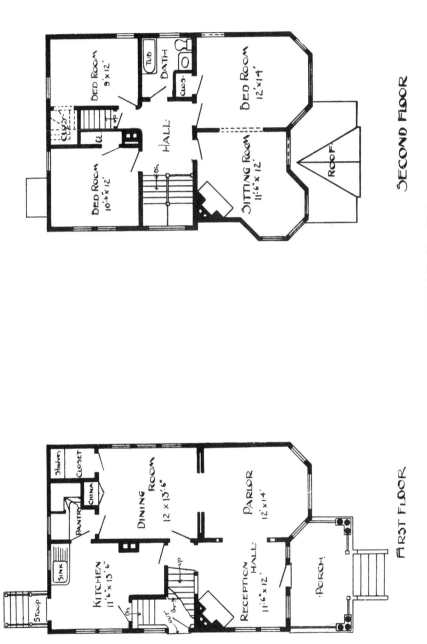

FIRST FLOOR

SECOND FLOOR

DESCRIPTION OF DESIGN No. 719.

GENERAL DIMENSIONS.—Length, 42 ft. over front porch; width, 25 ft. 3 in. Height of stories: cellar, 7 ft.; first story, 9 ft.; second story, 8 ft. 6 in.

EXTERIOR MATERIALS.—Foundation, stone; three courses of 10-inch ashlar above grade. Cellar under whole house, cemented throughout and divided by brick partitions into coal and furnace room, vegetable and fruit cellar. Ash pits under fireplaces. Whole house sheathed with ⅞-inch matched sheathing and covered with building paper and ½-inch lap siding, red wood shingles and slate roof as shown.

INTERIOR FINISH.—Three coats of plaster. All rooms on first floor with exception of kitchen finished in select quartered white oak, balance of building in yellow pine. All finished natural in three coat work and all of the several parts detailed. Doors and windows of good size and design. Combination stairs from kitchen to landing can be nicely arranged.

ACCOMMODATIONS.—Sizes of all rooms, location of closets, fixtures, etc., as shown on plans.

COST.—The contract cost, complete, $2,300. Price of working drawings, details, specifications, etc., all in duplicate, and license to build, $40.00.

DESIGN No. 720.

Cost, $3,300, complete.

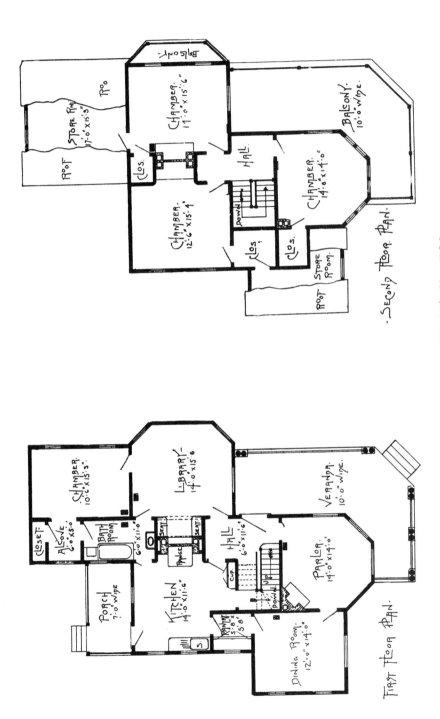

- Second Floor Plan.

First Floor Plan.

DESCRIPTION OF DESIGN No. 720.

GENERAL DIMENSIONS.—Width, 42 ft. 6 in.; length over porch, 60 ft. Height of stories: cellar, 7 ft.; first story, 9 ft. 2 in.; second story, 8 ft. 4 in.

EXTERIOR MATERIALS.—Foundation, stone; three courses of 10-inch ashlar above grade; cellar cemented. Ash pits under fire-places. Whole house sheathed with ⅞-inch matched sheathing and Neponset building paper. Building covered with ½-inch lap siding. Slate roof. Paint, three coats.

INTERIOR FINISH.—Three coats of plaster; whitewood finish throughout, except hall and stairs, which are of quartered white oak. Oak floors in hall, dining room and library. Maple floors in pantry, kitchen and bath room. All inside and outside finish detailed. All doors and windows of good size and specially designed.

ACCOMMODATIONS.—Sizes of all rooms and location of closets, pantries and fixtures as shown on the plans. The fire-place and nook off library is a very pleasing and cosy feature. Building heated by furnace. Hot and cold water plumbing, laundry, bath, etc.

COST.—The cost of this building is $3,300, complete.

Price of working plans, details, specifications, etc., all in duplicate, and license to build, $45.00.

DESIGN No. 721.
Cost, $2,500, complete.

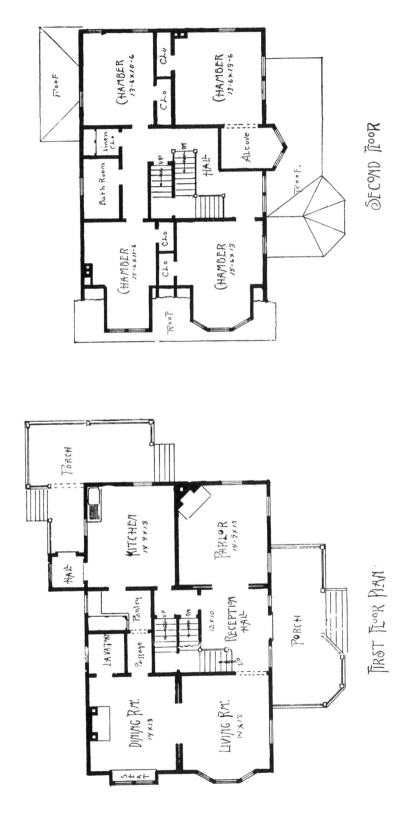

FIRST FLOOR PLAN

SECOND FLOOR

DESCRIPTION OF DESIGN No. 721.

GENERAL DIMENSIONS.—Length, 42 ft.; width, 44 ft. 6 in. Height of stories: cellar, 7 ft.; first story, 9 ft. 2 in.; second story, 8 ft. 6 in.

EXTERIOR MATERIALS.—Foundation, stone; three courses of 10-inch ashlar above grade. Cellar under whole, cemented, and divided into three rooms by brick division walls. Whole house sheathed with ⅞-inch matched sheathing and Neponset building paper, and covered with ½-inch lap siding and shingles as shown. Three coats of paint.

INTERIOR FINISH.—Three coats of plaster. Pine and whitewood finish throughout. Hardwood floors in kitchen and pantry. All doors and windows of good size and design.

ACCOMMODATIONS.—Sizes of all rooms and location of closets, fixtures, etc., as shown on plans. Building heated by furnace. Hot and cold water, plumbing, bath, etc.

COST.—Complete, $2,500. Price of working drawings, details, specifications, etc., all in duplicate, and license to build, $40.00.

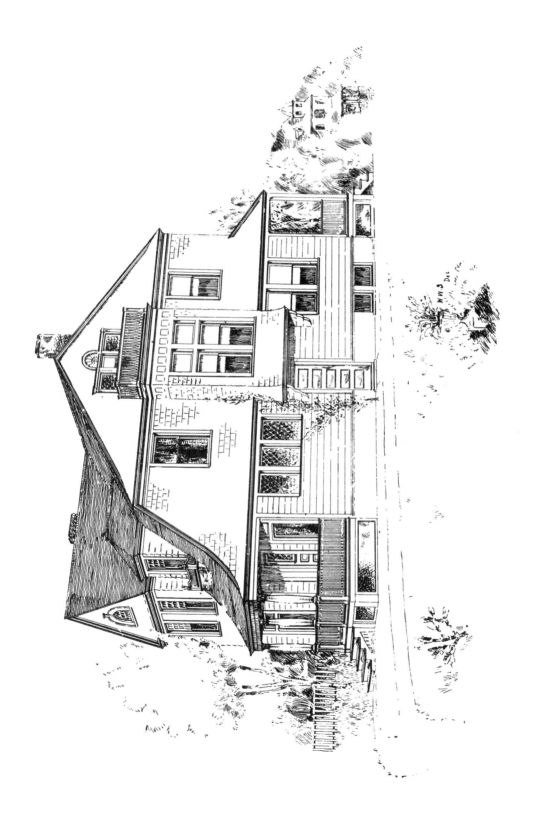

DESIGN No. 722.

Cost, $2,200, complete.

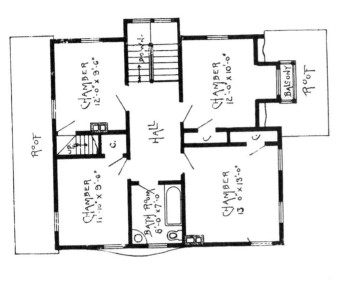

SECOND FLOOR PLAN

FIRST FLOOR PLAN

DESCRIPTION OF DESIGN No. 722.

GENERAL DIMENSIONS.—Width over bay, 29 ft. 3 in. Length over porch, 41 ft. Height of stories: cellar, 7 ft.; first story, 9 ft.; second story, 8 ft. 6 in.

EXTERIOR MATERIALS.—Foundation, stone; three courses of 8-inch ashlar above grade. Cellar under whole house, cemented throughout. Ash pits under fireplaces. Whole house sheathed with ⅞-inch matched sheathing and Neponset building paper. Dwelling covered with ½-inch lap siding and dipped shingles as shown. Three coats of paint.

INTERIOR FINISH.—Three coats of plaster. Finish, Georgia pine in reception hall, parlor and dining room, balance whitewood finish throughout. First floor finished natural. Second story stained to suit owner. All inside finish specially detailed. Doors and windows all of good size and special designs.

ACCOMMODATIONS.—Sizes of all rooms and location of closets, pantry and fixtures as shown on the plans. Building heated by furnace. Hot and cold water, plumbing, bath, etc.

COST.—The cost of this building, complete, was $2,200. Price of working plans, details, specifications, etc., all in duplicate, and license to build, $36.00.

DESIGN No. 723.

Cost, $2,300, complete.

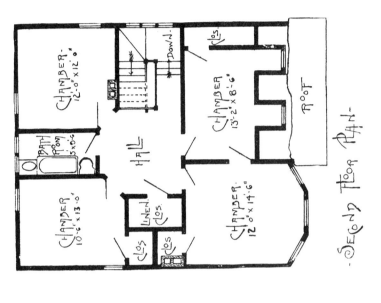

-SECOND FLOOR PLAN-

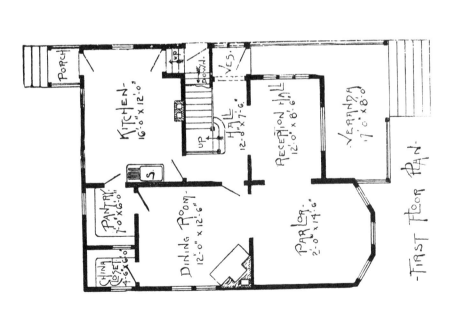

-FIRST FLOOR PLAN-

DESCRIPTION OF DESIGN No. 723.

GENERAL DIMENSIONS.—Width, 29 ft. 6 in.; length over porch, 38 ft. Height of stories: cellar, 7 ft.; first story, 9 ft.; second story, 8 ft. 6 in.

EXTERIOR MATERIALS.—Foundation, stone; three courses of 10-inch ashlar above grade. Cellar under whole house, cemented throughout. Ash pit under fire-place. Whole house sheathed with ⅞-inch matched sheathing and Neponset building paper. Dwelling covered as shown with dipped shingles and siding. Three coats of paint.

INTERIOR FINISH.—Three coats of plaster. Pine finish throughout; the lower floor finished natural. Balance of dwelling stained to suit owner. All finish detailed. Doors and windows all of good size and special design.

ACCOMMODATIONS.—Sizes of all rooms, with location of closets, pantry and fixtures as shown on the plans. All rooms are of ample size and well lighted, and this arrangement is such that gives a whole front in rooms unbroken, at the same time giving a front entrance and desirable hall. Building heated by furnace. Hot and cold water plumbing, laundry, bath, etc.

COST.—The cost complete is $2,300.

Price of working plans, details, specifications, etc., all in duplicate and license to build, $38.00.

DESIGN No. 724.

Cost, $1,850, complete.

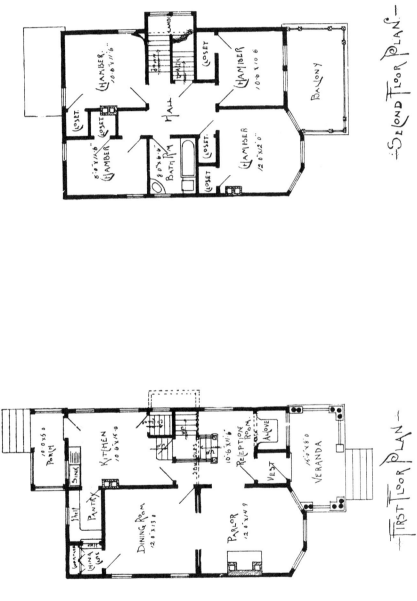

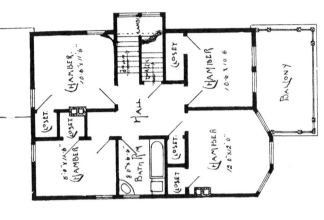

DESCRIPTION OF DESIGN No. 724.

General Dimensions.—Width, 24 ft. Length over porch, 40 ft. 6 in. Height of stories: cellar, 7 ft.; first story, 9 ft. 2 in.; second story, 8 ft. 4 in.

Exterior Materials.—Foundation, stone; three courses of 8-inch ashlar above grade. Cellar under whole house and cemented throughout. Ash pits under fireplaces. Whole house sheathed with ⅞-inch matched sheathing. Dwelling covered as shown with ½-inch lap siding and dipped shingles. Slate roof. Two coats of paint.

Interior Finish.—Three coats of plaster. Pine finish throughout, finished to suit owner. All finish detailed. Doors and windows all of good size.

Accommodations.—Sizes of all rooms, with the location of closets, pantry, etc., with fixtures, are shown on plan. All rooms are of ample size and this is a design we would recommend to parties who would wish a house for something less than $2,000, as it is desirable in arrangement and neat and homelike in appearance. Building heated by furnace. Hot and cold water, plumbing, bath, etc.

Cost.—The cost, complete, is $1,850. Price of working plans, details, specifications, etc., all in duplicate, and license to build, $32.00.

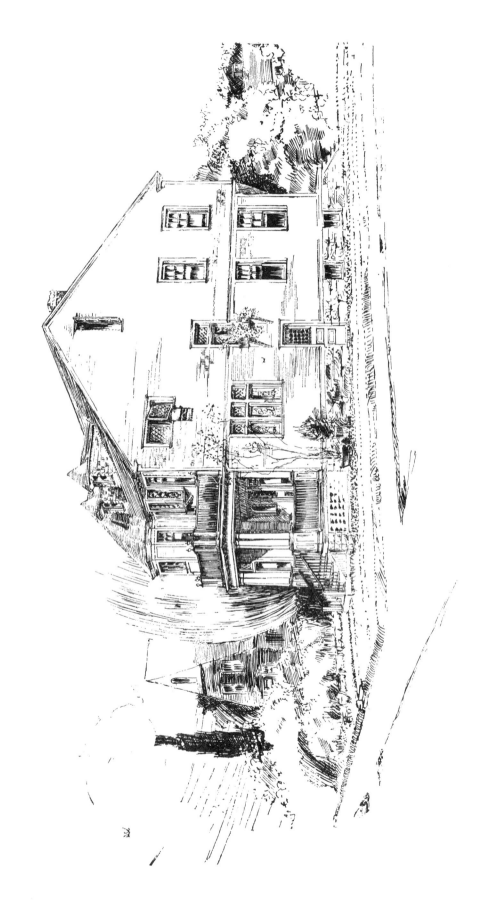

DESIGN No. 725.

Cost, $2,500, complete.

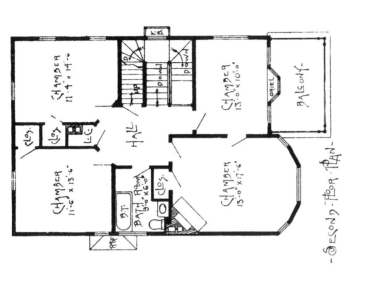

-SECOND FLOOR PLAN-

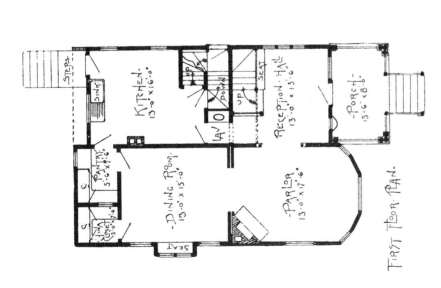

FIRST FLOOR PLAN-

DESCRIPTION OF DESIGN No. 725.

GENERAL DIMENSIONS.—Width, 29 ft.; length, 44 ft. 6 in. Height of stories: cellar, 7 ft.; first story, 9 ft. 2 in.; second story, 8 ft. 4 in.

EXTERIOR MATERIALS.—Foundation, stone; three courses of 10-inch ashlar above grade. Cellar ceiling plastered, and floors cemented throughout. Ash pits under all fire-places. Whole house sheathed with ⅞-inch matched sheathing and Neponset building paper. First and second stories covered as shown, roof slated with blue slate. Three coats of paint.

INTERIOR FINISH.—Three coats of plaster; hardwood finish in front chambers and reception hall, with finely carved newel on the staircase; balance in whitewood or yellow pine, finished natural. All inside and outside finish detailed. All doors and windows of good size and specially designed.

ACCOMMODATIONS.—Sizes of all rooms, and location of closets, pantries and fixtures, as shown on the plans. Such features as window seats, etc., are also shown, which makes this plan one of the most satisfactory, having many of the latest desirable features. Building heated by furnace. Hot and cold water plumbing, laundry, bath, etc.

COST.—The cost of this design as from our specifications was $2,500, complete.

Price for working plans, details, specifications, etc., in duplicate, and license to build, $38.00.

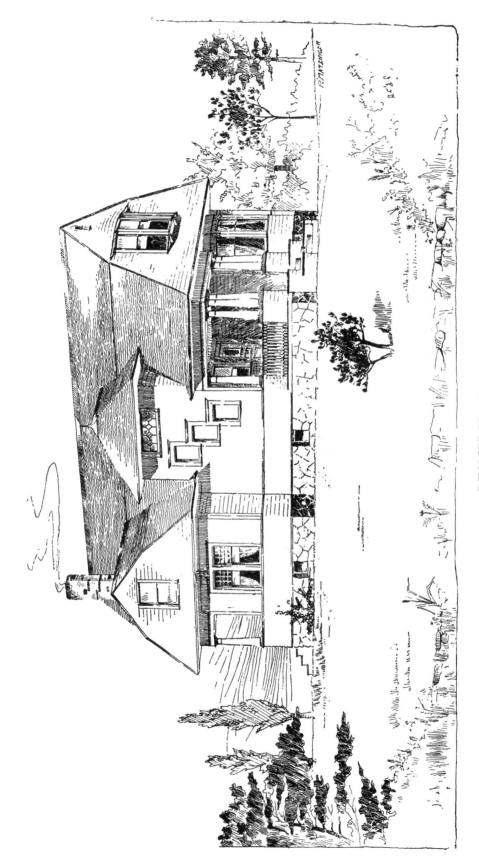

DESIGN No. 726.

Cost, $1,800, complete.

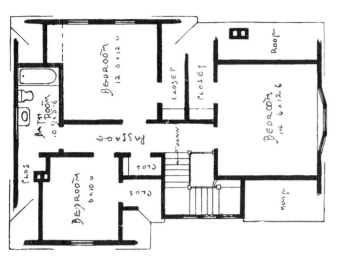

— SECOND·FLOOR·PLAN —

— FIRST·FLOOR·PLAN —

DESCRIPTION OF DESIGN No. 726.

GENERAL DIMENSIONS.—Length, 39 ft. 6 in. over front porch and parlor bay ; width, 27 ft. 6 in. over dining room bay. Height of stories ; cellar, 7 ft.; first story, 9 ft.; second story, 8 ft. 6 in.

EXTERIOR MATERIALS.—Foundation, stone ; three courses of nine-inch ashlar above grade. Cellar under whole house, cemented throughout. Same has necessary coal bins, shelving, etc. Ash pit under fireplace. Whole house sheathed with ⅞-inch matched sheathing and Neponset building paper. Building covered with ½-inch lap siding, California redwood shingles. Two coats of paint.

INTERIOR FINISH.—Three coats of plaster. Reception hall and staircase finished in oak, balance of dwelling in select yellow pine and whitewood, stained or finished natural to suit owner. Hardwood floors in reception hall, kitchen, pantry, bath room and alcove. All finish for the several parts detailed. All doors and windows of good size and design. Front door veneered with quartered oak and glazed with ¼-inch beveled American plate glass. All windows glazed with select double American or leaded glass.

ACCOMMODATIONS.—Sizes of all rooms, location of closets, fixtures, etc., as shown on plans. Building heated by furnace. Hot and cold water, plumbing, bath, etc.

COST.—The contract cost, complete, $1,800. Price of working drawings, all details, specifications, etc., all in duplicate, and license to build, $30.00.

DESIGN No. 727.

Cost, $1,600, complete.

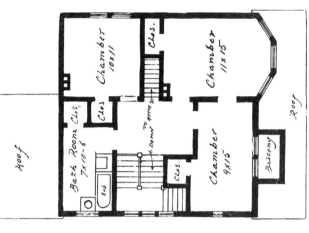

SECOND FLOOR PLAN.

FIRST FLOOR PLAN.

DESCRIPTION OF DESIGN No. 727.

GENERAL DIMENSIONS.—Width, 27 ft. 6 in.; length, 44 ft. 6 in. Height of stories: cellar, 6 ft.; first story, 9 ft.; second story, 8 ft.

EXTERIOR MATERIALS.—Foundation, stone; three courses of 10-inch ashlar above grade. Cellar under whole, cemented throughout and divided with ceiled partitions. Whole house sheathed with ⅞-inch sheathing, matched, and Neponset building paper, and covered with ½-inch lap siding and dipped shingles as shown. Two coats of paint.

INTERIOR FINISH.—Three coats of plaster. Yellow pine finish throughout. Kitchen, pantry, rear hall and bath wainscoted 3 ft. 6 in. high. Kitchen and pantry floored with 2-inch by ⅞-inch maple flooring. All doors and windows of good size and design.

ACCOMMODATIONS.—Sizes of all rooms and location of closets, fixtures, etc., as shown on plans. Cellar arranged for coal, furnace, laundry and vegetable room. Building heated by furnace. Hot and cold water plumbing, bath, etc.

COST.—Cost, $1,600, complete.

Price of working drawings, details, specifications, etc., all in duplicate, and license to build, $28.00.

DESIGN No. 728.

Cost, $2,300, complete.

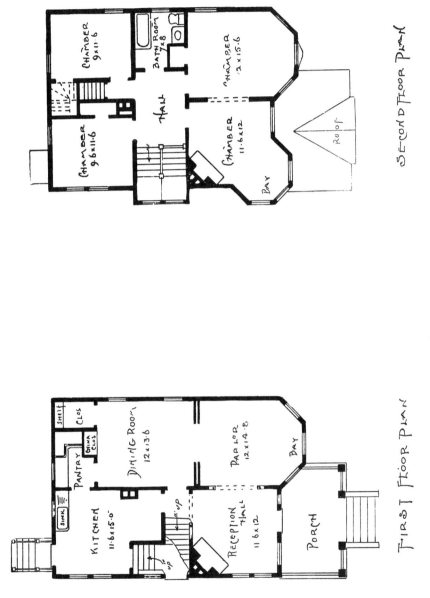

FIRST FLOOR PLAN

SECOND FLOOR PLAN

DESCRIPTION OF DESIGN No. 728.

GENERAL DIMENSIONS.—Length, 41 ft. 6 in. over front porch; width, 25 ft. Height of stories: cellar, 7 ft.; first story, 9 ft. 2 in.; second story, 8 ft. 4 in.

EXTERIOR MATERIALS.—Foundation, stone; three courses of 10-inch ashlar above grade. Cellar under whole house, divided by 8-inch brick partitions into furnace and coal room, laundry and vegetable cellar. Ash pit under fire-place. Whole house sheathed with ⅞-inch matched sheathing and Neponset building paper. Building covered with ½-inch lap siding, dipped dimensioned shingles and slate roof as shown. Three coats of paint.

INTERIOR FINISH.—Three coats of plaster. Reception hall, staircase, parlor and dining room finished in select oak. Balance of house in select white pine. All finished natural and all parts detailed. Oak floors in reception hall and dining room. Select maple flooring in kitchen, pantry and bath room. All doors are of five horizontal panel designs. Outside and sliding doors are 1¾-inch thick. Front door to be as detailed, of veneered quartered white oak. Windows glazed with select double American and leaded glass.

ACCOMMODATIONS.—Sizes of all rooms, location of closets, fixtures, etc., as shown on plans. Combination stair arrangement from kitchen can be easily and satisfactorily made. Building heated by furnace. Hot and cold water plumbing, laundry, bath, etc.

COST.—Contract cost complete, $2,300.

Price of working drawings, all details, specifications, etc., all in duplicate, and license to build, $35.00.

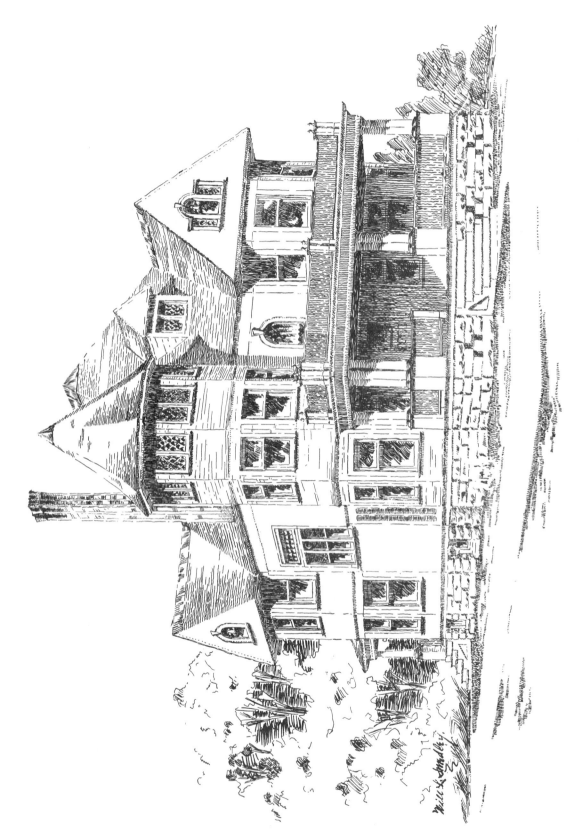

DESIGN No. 729.

Cost, $3,500, complete.

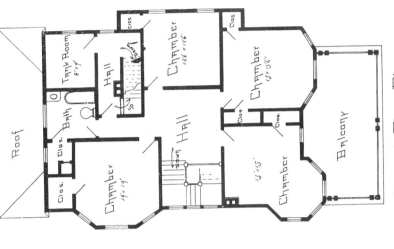

Second Floor Plan

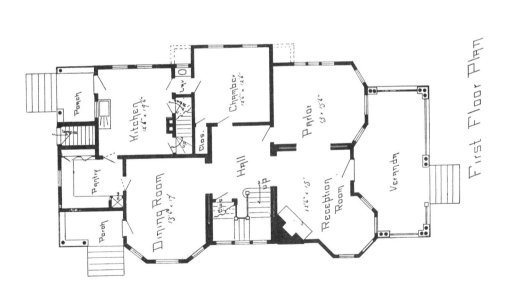

First Floor Plan

DESCRIPTION OF DESIGN No. 729.

GENERAL DIMENSIONS.—Length, 63 ft. over veranda. Veranda, 13 ft. in width. Width, 36 ft. Height of stories: cellar, 7 ft.; first story, 9 ft. 2 in.: second story, 8 ft. 6 in.

EXTERIOR MATERIALS.—Foundation of stone; four courses of 9-inch ashlar above grade; brick partitions in basement. Whole house sheathed with ⅞-inch matched sheathing and covered with Neponset building paper and ½-inch lap siding. Chimneys of pressed brick, and building painted three coats.

INTERIOR FINISH.—Cellar cemented throughout and with plastered ceiling. Three coats of plaster throughout the building, including attic. Quartered white oak floors with border, and quartered white oak finish in reception room, hall and dining room; maple floors in pantry, kitchen, lavatory and bath room. White enamel finish in parlor. Balance of house in yellow pine finish. All wood work, except in parlor, finished natural in four coat work. All finish detailed. Doors and windows of good size.

ACCOMMODATIONS.—Cellar under entire building, divided into vegetable and store rooms, laundry, coal and furnace room. Building heated by hot air furnace. Laundry fitted out with wash trays, etc. Hot and cold water plumbing throughout. Lavatory, kitchen and bath room fitted with all fixtures as shown. Linen closet off bath room. Dumb waiter from basement to attic, opening into pantry on first floor and linen closet on second floor. Rear stairs and outside cellar entrance. All chambers have ample closet room. One chamber finished in attic.

COST.—$3,500, complete. Price of working drawings, specifications, etc., all in duplicate, all details and license to build, $50.00.

DESIGN No. 730.

Cost, $4,000, complete.

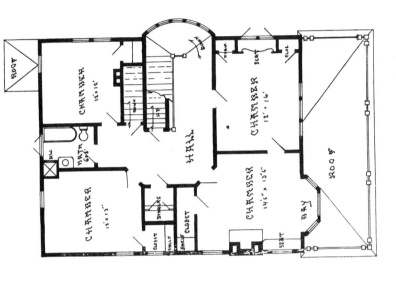

SECOND FLOOR PLAN

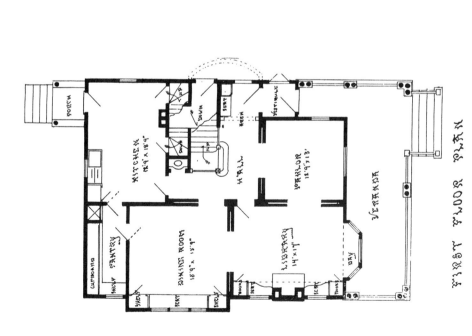

FIRST FLOOR PLAN

DESCRIPTION OF DESIGN No. 730.

GENERAL DIMENSIONS.—Length, 49 ft. 6 in. over front veranda ; veranda 12 ft. in width ; width, 34 ft. Height of stories : cellar, 7 ft. ; first story, 9 ft. 2 in. ; second story, 8 ft. 6 in.

EXTERIOR MATERIALS.—Foundation of stone, three courses of 12-inch ashlar above grade ; brick partitions in basement. Whole house sheathed with ⅞-inch matched sheathing and covered with Neponset building paper and ½-inch lap siding. Roofs of black slate. Chimneys of pressed brick, and building painted three coats.

INTERIOR FINISH.—Cellar cemented throughout and with plastered ceiling. Three coats of plaster throughout the building, including attic. Quartered white oak floors with border, and quartered white oak finish in vestibule, hall and dining room ; maple floors in pantry, kitchen and bath room. White enamel finish in parlor ; quartered sycamore finish in library ; balance of house in yellow pine finish. All woodwork, except in parlor, finished in four coat work. Special features are shown in the way of seats and book cases in library, and window seat and china closets in dining room. A pretty seat and table is also shown in hall. All finish detailed. Doors and windows of good size.

ACCOMMODATIONS.—Cellar under entire building, divided into vegetable and store rooms, laundry, coal and furnace room. Building heated by hot air furnace. Laundry fitted out with wash trays, etc. Hot and cold water plumbing throughout. Lavatory, kitchen and bath room fitted with all fixtures as shown. Linen closet off bath room. Dumb waiter from basement to attic, opening into pantry on first floor and bath room on second floor. Rear stairs and outside cellar entrance. All chambers have ample closet room. One chamber finished in attic.

COST.—$4,000, complete. Price of working drawings, specifications, etc., all in duplicate, all details and license to build, $56.00.

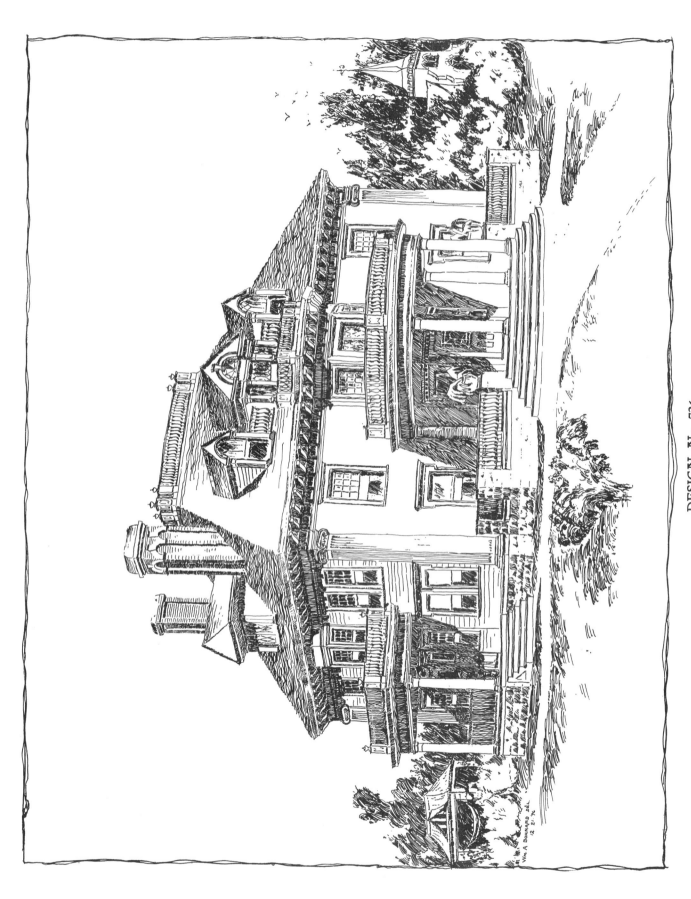

DESIGN No. 731.

Cost, $4,500, complete.

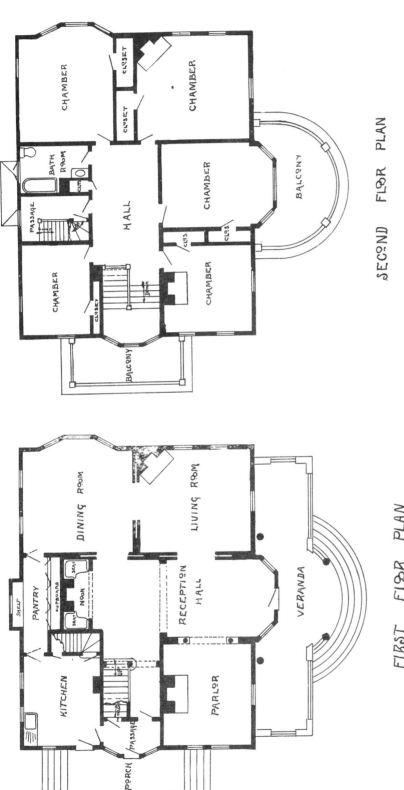

FIRST FLOOR PLAN

SECOND FLOOR PLAN

DESCRIPTION OF DESIGN No. 731.

GENERAL DIMENSIONS.—Length, 53 ft. over veranda. Veranda, 10 ft. in width. Width, 56 ft. over porch. Porch, 8 ft. in width. Height of stories: cellar, 7 ft.; first story, 9 ft. 2 in.; second story, 8 ft. 6 in.

EXTERIOR MATERIALS.—Foundation of stone; three courses of 12-inch ashlar above grade; brick partitions in basement. Whole house sheathed with ⅞-inch matched sheathing and covered with Neponset building paper and ½-inch lap siding. Roofs of black slate. Chimneys of pressed brick, and building painted three coats.

INTERIOR FINISH.—Cellar cemented throughout, and with plastered ceiling. Three coats of plaster throughout the building, including attic. Quartered white oak floors with border, and quartered white oak finish in reception hall, passage, nook, living room and dining room; maple floors in pantry, kitchen, upper passage and bath room. White enamel finish in parlor. Balance of house in yellow pine finish. All wood work, except in parlor, finished natural in four coat work. Special column features between rear hall and parlor and to stairway, also nook in reception hall. All finish detailed. Doors and windows of good size.

ACCOMMODATIONS.—Cellar under entire building, divided into vegetable and store rooms, laundry, coal and furnace room. Building heated by hot air furnace. Laundry fitted out with wash trays, etc. Hot and cold water plumbing throughout. Kitchen and bath room fitted with all fixtures as shown. Rear stairs as shown coming into passage on second floor, with attic stairs over same, making an arrangement whereby servant's quarters can be closed off from second floor. All chambers have ample closet room. One chamber finished in attic.

COST.—$4,500, complete. Price of working drawings, specifications, etc., all in duplicate, all details and license to build, $60.00.

DESIGN No. 732.

Cost, $4,200, complete.

Second Floor Plan

First Floor Plan

DESCRIPTION OF DESIGN No. 732.

GENERAL DIMENSIONS.—Length, 60 ft.; width; width, 35 ft. Height of stories: cellar, 7 ft.; first story, 9 ft. 2 in.; second story, 8 ft. 6 in.

EXTERIOR MATERIALS.—Foundation of stone; four courses of 9-inch ashlar above grade; brick partitions in basement. Whole house sheathed with ⅞-inch matched sheathing and covered with Neponset building paper and ½-inch lap siding. Roofs of black slate. Chimneys of pressed brick, and building painted three coats.

INTERIOR FINISH.—Cellar cemented throughout and with plastered ceiling. Three coats of plaster throughout the building, including attic. Quartered white oak floors with border, and quartered white oak finish in vestibule, reception room, hall, lavatory, rear hall and dining room; maple floors in pantry, kitchen and bath room. White enamel finish in parlor and front chambers and lavatory on second floor; cherry finish in library; balance of house in yellow pine finish. All woodwork, except in parlor, finished natural in four coat work. All finish detailed and hardwood rubbed. Doors and windows of good size.

ACCOMMODATIONS.—Cellar under entire building, divided into vegetable and store rooms, laundry, coal and furnace room. Building heated by hot air furnace. Laundry fitted with wash trays, etc. Hot and cold water plumbing throughout. Lavatory, kitchen and bath room fitted with all fixtures as shown. Linen closet off upper rear hall. Dumb waiter from basement to attic, opening into pantry and kitchen on first floor and linen closet on second floor. Rear stairs and cellar entrance from rear hall. All chambers have ample closet room. One chamber finished in attic. Special features are shown with delightful seat in hall, also niche for statuary, seat in dining room and book case in library.

COST.—$4,200, complete. Price of working drawings, specifications, etc., all in duplicate, all details and license to build, $56.00.

DESIGN No. 733.

Cost, $3,700, complete.

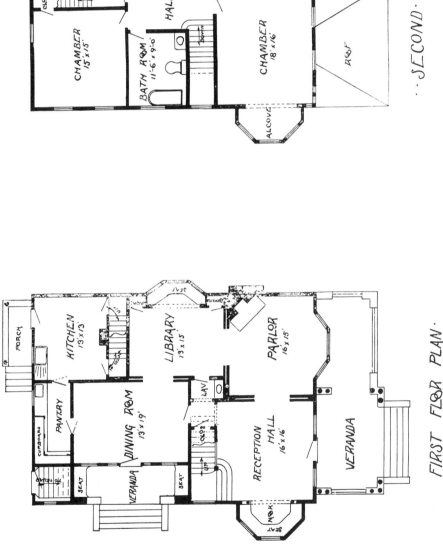

..SECOND..FLOOR..PLAN.

FIRST FLOOR PLAN.

DESCRIPTION OF DESIGN No. 733.

GENERAL DIMENSIONS.—Length, 50 ft. over veranda. Veranda, 13 ft. in width. Width, 42 ft. Height of stories: cellar, 7 ft.; first story, 9 ft. 2 in.; second story, 8 ft. 6 in.

EXTERIOR MATERIALS.—Foundation of stone; three courses of 12-inch ashlar above grade; brick partitions in basement. Whole house sheathed with ⅞-inch matched sheathing, and covered with Neponset building paper and ½-inch lap siding. Roofs of black slate. Chimneys of pressed brick; and building painted three coats.

INTERIOR FINISH.—Cellar cemented throughout, and with plastered ceiling. Three coats of plaster throughout the building, including attic. Quartered white oak floors with border, and quartered white oak finish in reception hall, nook and dining room; maple floors in pantry, kitchen, lavatory and bath room. Cherry or birch finish stained mahogany in parlor and library; upper front chambers in white and blue. Balance of house in yellow pine finish. All wood work, except in white, finished natural in four coat work. All finish detailed, and hardwood rubbed. Doors and windows of good size.

ACCOMMODATIONS.—Cellar under entire building, divided into vegetable and store rooms, laundry, coal and furnace room. Building heated by hot air furnace. Laundry fitted out with wash trays, etc. Hot and cold water plumbing throughout. Lavatory, kitchen and bath room fitted with all fixtures as shown. Rear stairs and outside cellar entrance. All chambers have ample closet room. One chamber finished in attic. Special features are shown : delightful nook and seat of seat, seats on each side of seat, seats on side veranda, and an alcove off upper chamber.

COST.—$3,700, complete. Price of working drawings, specifications, etc., all in duplicate, all details and license to build, $50.00.

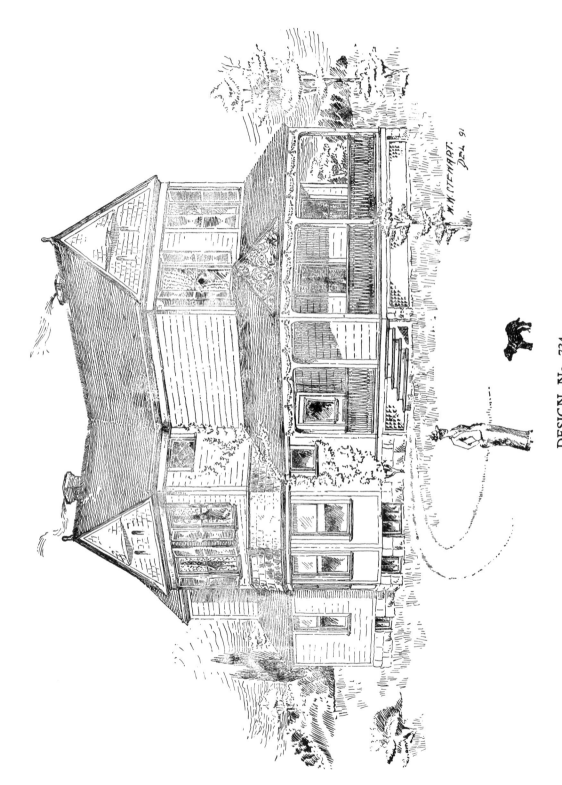

DESIGN No. 734.

Cost, $1,600, complete.

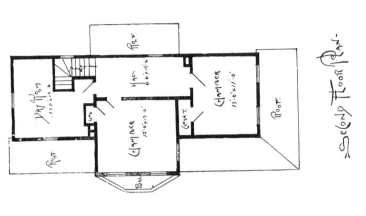

DESCRIPTION OF DESIGN No. 734.

GENERAL DIMENSIONS.—Width, over bays, 27 ft. Length, over porch, 47 ft. 6 in. Height of stories: cellar, 7 ft.; first story, 9 ft.; second story, 8 ft. 6 in.

EXTERIOR MATERIALS.—Foundation, stone; two courses of 12-inch ashlar above grade. Cellar cemented. Ash-pit under fire-place. Whole house sheathed with ⅞-inch matched sheathing, and covered with ½-inch lap siding and shingles as shown. Two coats of paint.

INTERIOR FINISH.—Two coats of plaster and yellow pine finish throughout. All finish taken from stock designs and painted and stained to suit owner. Doors and windows all of good size.

ACCOMMODATIONS.—Size of rooms, location of closets and fixtures as shown on plans. This house built according to our plans will be sure to cost less than more pretentious houses. Including hot and cold water plumbing and furnace.

COST.—$1,600, complete. Price of working plans, details, specifications, etc., all in duplicate and license to build, $25.00.

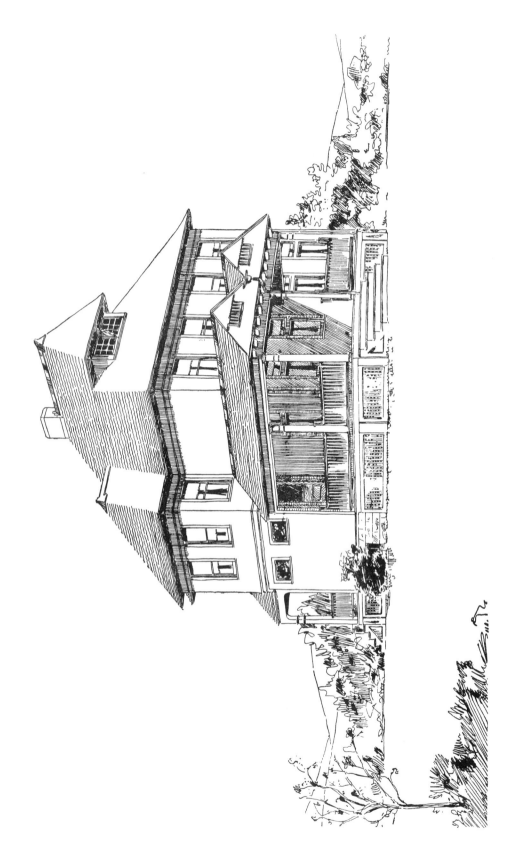

DESIGN No. 735.

Cost, $2,100, complete.

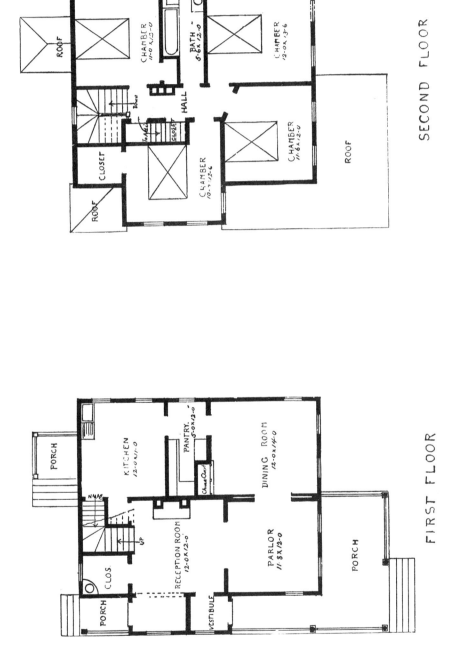

SECOND FLOOR

FIRST FLOOR

DESCRIPTION OF DESIGN No. 735.

GENERAL DIMENSIONS.—Length, 32 ft.; width, 31 ft. Height of stories: cellar, 7 ft.; first story, 9 ft.; second story, 8 ft. 6 in.

EXTERIOR MATERIALS.—Foundation, stone; three courses of 10-inch ashlar above grade. Cellar under whole house, cemented throughout, and divided into two rooms by brick partition. Outside cellar entrance under main stairs. Ash pit under fireplace. Whole house sheathed with ⅞-inch matched sheathing and Neponset building paper, and covered with ½-inch lap pine siding, and slate roof as shown.

INTERIOR FINISH.—Three coats of plaster. Reception hall, parlor and dining room finished in select white oak; balance of dwelling in yellow pine. All finished natural in three coat work and all of the several parts detailed. Hardwood floors in reception hall, closet, kitchen, pantry and bath room. Closet, kitchen, pantry and bath room wainscoted four feet high. Doors and windows of good size and design. All outside doors 1¾ inches thick. Front door and side door veneered with quartered oak and glazed with beveled American plate. All windows glazed with select double American and leaded glass.

ACCOMMODATIONS.—Sizes of all rooms, location of closets, fixtures, etc., as shown on plans. Door or archway can be arranged between reception room and dining room. Building is heated by hot air furnace. Hot and cold water plumbing throughout. Laundry fitted with wash trays, etc. Bath room has all necessary fixtures.

COST.—$2,100, complete. Price of working drawings, all details, specifications, etc., all in duplicate, and license to build, $36.00.

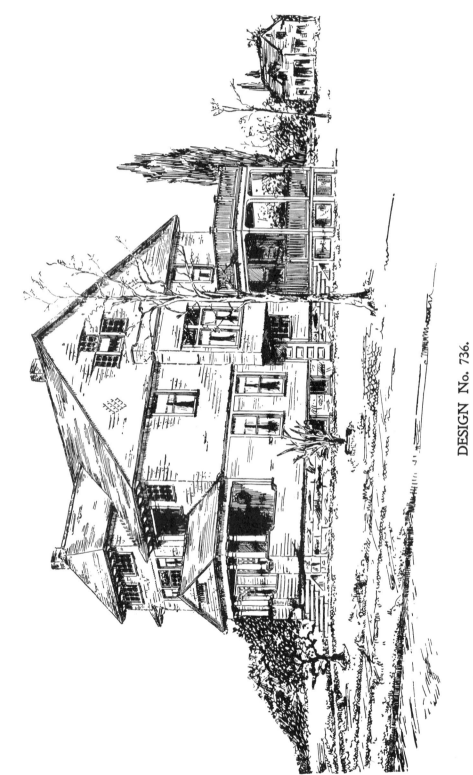

DESIGN No. 736.

Cost, $2,400, complete.

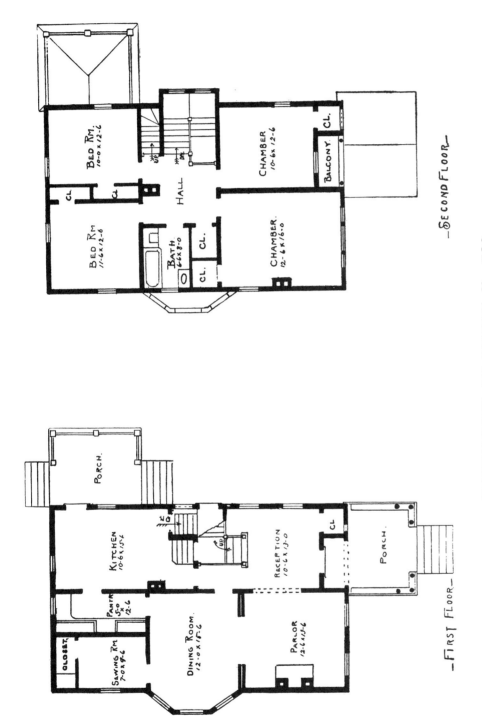

—Second Floor—

—First Floor—

DESCRIPTION OF DESIGN No. 736.

General Dimensions.—Length, 40 ft.; width, 27 ft. 6 in. Height of stories: cellar, 7 ft.; first story, 9 ft. 2 in.; second story, 8 ft. 4 in.

Exterior Materials.—Foundation, stone; three courses of 10-inch ashlar above grade. Cellar under whole house, cemented throughout, and having the necessary coal bins, shelving, etc. Outside cellar entrance under stair-case bay. Ash pit under fire-place. Whole house sheathed with ⅞-inch matched sheathing, and Neponset building paper, and covered with ½-inch lap siding, and dipped shingles and slate roof as shown.

Interior Finish.—Three coats of plaster. All inside finish of the several parts as detailed, of yellow pine. All finished natural in three coat work. Hardwood floors in reception hall, kitchen, pantry, and bath-room. Kitchen, pantry and bath-room wainscoted four feet high. Doors and windows of good size and design, and all windows glazed with select double American glass. Front outside door, 1¾ inches thick, of veneered white oak, glazed with beveled American plate glass.

Accommodations.—Sizes of all rooms, location of closets, fixtures, etc., as shown on plans. Building heated by hot air furnace. Hot and cold water plumbing throughout. Laundry fitted with wash trays, etc. Bath-room has all necessary fixtures.

Cost.—Cost, $2,400, complete. Price of working drawings, all details, specifications, etc., all in duplicate and license to build, $36.00.

Note.—This building was put up above the foundation as above described, in Massachusetts, for $1,660.

INTENDING BUILDERS.

We have had much to do with the development of domestic architecture, which has wonderfully improved in the last few years, the public having become more educated to the beauty of home buildings of the cheapest kinds, and there is no reason why in this enlightened era, one should not have an artistic and pretty building, when the cost is no more in erecting such than the old style houses.

Beautiful buildings have been the cause of ready sale to all adjoining property to that which they occupy, they have enhanced the value of their own sites, and all in their immediate neighborhood, and one can always note the ready sale such buildings, embodying the proper arrangements and conveniences, have, and at always a handsome profit, and this is the class of work we do.

CAUTION. ❧ ❧ ❧ ❧ ❧ ❧

The publishers of this work are protected by the Copyright Laws of the United States, and hereby warn all persons that no plan or portion of plan represented herein may be copied or used without permission of the publishers.

NOTICE. ❧ ❧ ❧ ❧ ❧ ❧

Persons using a design once have had value received, and any one using designs that have been used once, either the original or a copy, are using the architect's property, and it is held by the highest courts that pay can be collected for the use of said designs for every time they are employed.

When we furnish drawings to a party we always insert in specifications that said drawings must be returned to architects, (unless otherwise agreed upon), so as to avoid any chance of using them the second time. But we find, in many instances, that instructions in that respect are not followed, but our designs are sold to some one else, and are used over and over again. This we cannot allow; these designs are our property, and placing them on cloth or paper for the use of same, does not imply that we give them away for every one to use. We simply loan them to the party for a *consideration.* This is different from publishing a design and not copyrighting it. When this is done it is supposed to be the same as a gift to the public, and all can employ it free of cost.

THE FOX FURNACE.

FOX, VAUGHN & CO., Selling Agents, 61 Prospect St.

"THE BEST THAT CAN BE PURCHASED AT ANY PRICE."

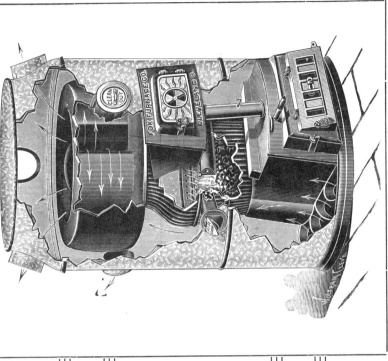

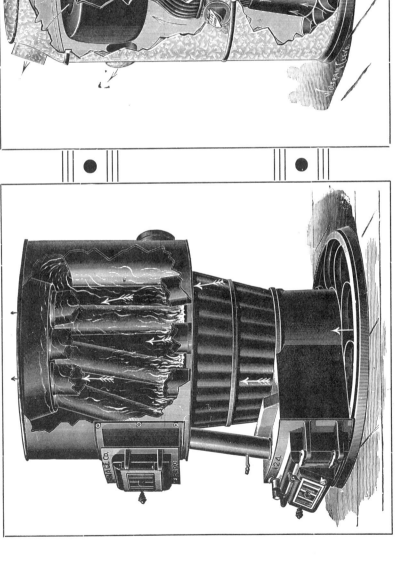

The Fox Furnace Co.,

Manufacturers,

CLEVELAND, OHIO.

Catalogues and Prices

for the asking. . . . . .

AULD & CONGER,

SLATE ROOFING CONTRACTORS.

ESTIMATES FURNISHED ON APPLICATION FOR ALL KINDS

OF SLATE ROOFING, BLACKBOARDS, ETC.

HIGHEST AWARD AT

. . . ON . . . .

THE WORLD'S FAIR

BANGOR ROOFING SLATE,

MINED FROM

The Bangor Union Quarry, Auld, Conger & Co.,
Bangor, Pa.

HIGHEST AWARD AT

. . . ON . . .

THE WORLD'S FAIR

SEA GREEN ROOFING SLATE,

MINED FROM

The Mammoth Vein Quarries, Poultney, Vt.,
owned and operated by us.

Mantels, Grates and Tile,

Fire Place Trimmings . . .

———— *of all descriptions.*

TILE BATH ROOMS, WAINSCOTING
and FLOOR WORK A SPECIALTY.

AULD & CONGER,

262 PROSPECT STREET.

TELEPHONE MAIN 308.   Next to Y. M. C. A. Building.

ESTIMATES ————

PROMPTLY FURNISHED.

THE GEORGE WORTHINGTON HARDWARE CO.,
CLEVELAND, OHIO.

YALE & SARGENT LOCKS,
YALE & SARGENT BUILDERS' HARDWARE,
YALE & SARGENT ART METAL WORK.

—— UNEQUALED IN SECURITY, DESIGN, FINISH AND WORKMANSHIP. ——

PRICES AND GOODS TO SUIT ALL CONDITIONS.
LET US FIGURE YOUR BILL OF HARDWARE.

90

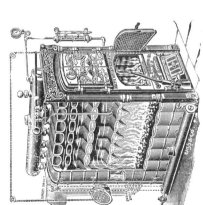
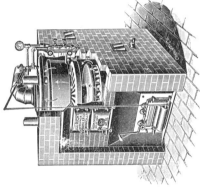

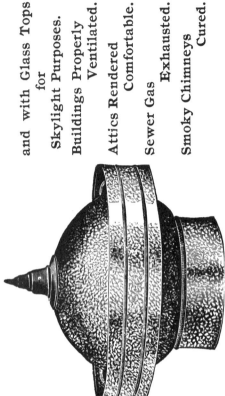
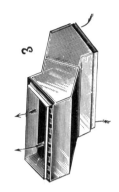
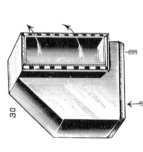
92

IVORY CEMENT,

...MANUFACTURED BY...

The Midland Plaster Co.,

KANSAS CITY, MO.

••••

This Cement is the perfection of HARD WALL PLASTERS, and is used for plastering walls or ceilings.

It is manufactured from the purest of gypsum, and for lath plaster contain the finest of washed hair or asbestos fibre; for brick walls it is used mixed only with sand.

For hardness, durability or cheapness it excels all plasters on the market, and when properly applied it makes a wall which is impossible to damage by water or heat. It works evenly and hardens to the density of marble.

This Cement is used by all leading contractors and builders.

••••

SOLD BY

The Cleveland Builders' Supply Co.,

733-734 Garfield Building,

CLEVELAND, OHIO.

The Garbage Problem Solved

Mann's Garbage Drier and Burner successfully collects all garbage from the house and disposes of it by fire. Designed for domestic use in private families or for flats, restaurants and hotels. Takes the place of a grease trap, catch basin, garbage box, and is a crematory for everything about the house that is to be destroyed.

Write for Descriptive Pamphlet and Prices to

GARDNER & MANN, Dowagiac, Mich.

DAVID FISK,

SHEET METAL WORKER.

Furnace Cleaning and Repairing, Roofing, Guttering and all Kinds of

——REPAIR WORK——

in my line promptly attended to.

Orders by mail will receive prompt attention.

Shop and Office 1340 Zoeter Avenue.

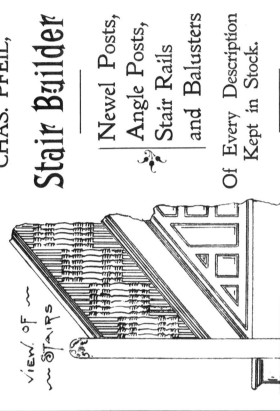
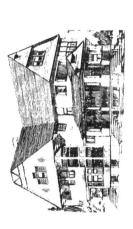

THE ROUSE & HILLS COMPANY,

53-55-57-59 Frankfort St., CLEVELAND, O.

Manufacturers of

Compression and Fuller Work, Lavatory and Bath Trimmings.

—————— FULL LINE OF ——————

WHITE ENAMELED BATHS

COLUMBIA
IDEAL
LUXURIA
VEDORA

Superior and Seneca Low Down Syphons,

Frankfort and Niagara Syphon Jet Closets.

TELEPHONE MAIN 1882.

THE FRANKFORT.